DOCUMENTS FROM MODERN RUSSIA

FIRST EDITION

EDITED BY

MARGARET PEACOCK and RICHARD B. SPENCE
University of Alabama – Tuscaloosa   University of Idaho

Bassim Hamadeh, CEO and Publisher
David Miano, Senior Acquisitions Editor
Michelle Piehl, Senior Project Editor
Alia Bales, Production Editor
Jess Estrella, Senior Graphic Designer
Greg Isales, Licensing Associate
Natalie Piccotti, Director of Marketing
Kassie Graves, Vice President of Editorial
Jamie Giganti, Director of Academic Publishing

Copyright © 2021 by Cognella, Inc. All rights reserved. No part of this publication may be reprinted, reproduced, transmitted, or utilized in any form or by any electronic, mechanical, or other means, now known or hereafter invented, including photocopying, microfilming, and recording, or in any information retrieval system without the written permission of Cognella, Inc. For inquiries regarding permissions, translations, foreign rights, audio rights, and any other forms of reproduction, please contact the Cognella Licensing Department at rights@cognella.com.

Trademark Notice: Product or corporate names may be trademarks or registered trademarks and are used only for identification and explanation without intent to infringe.

Cover: Copyright © 2017 Depositphotos/CamillaCasablanca.

Printed in the United States of America.

TABLE OF CONTENTS

Introduction		ix
Chapter 1: The Great Reforms, Imperial Expansion, and Tsarism under Attack, 1855–1881		1
Reading 1	Landlord and Peasant on the Eve of Emancipation, 1857–1859	2
Reading 2	The Edict of Emancipation, 1861	4
Reading 3	Emancipation's Aftermath, 1861	7
Reading 4	The Table of Ranks (Tabel' o Rangakh), 1722	9
Reading 5	Sergei Nechayev, 1869	11
Reading 6	Fyodor Dostoevsky, Slavophile Intellectual, 1877	14
Reading 7	Sir Donald Mackenzie Wallace's Observations on Russian Social Classes, 1870s	15
Chapter 2: Autocracy Retrenched and the Empire in Flux, 1881–1904		19
Reading 8	Konstantin Pobedonostsev's "Philosophy of Reaction," 1898	20
Reading 9	The "May Laws," 1882	22
Reading 10	Dostoevsky Praises Russian Imperialism, 1881	23
Reading 11	The Measure of Russian "Backwardness," 1880–1890	24
Reading 12	George Kennan on Political Exiles, 1891	26
Reading 13	The 1897 Russian Census, 1897	28
Chapter 3: The Disintegration of the Imperial Regime, 1905–1917		31
Reading 14	The Manifesto on the Improvement of the State Order, 1905	32

Reading 15	The Russian Fundamental Law of April 23, 1906 and the Powers of the Emperor, 1906	34
Reading 16	The Stolypin Reforms, 1906	36
Reading 17	Russian State Duma Elections, 1906–1912	39
Reading 18	Russia on the Eve of Armageddon, 1914	40
Reading 19	Pyotr Durnovo's Memorandum to Tsar Nicholas, 1914	44
Reading 20	Helphand-Parvus's Plan for Subversion in Russia, 1915	48
Reading 21	The Impact of WWI on Russia, 1917	50

Chapter 4: The Russian Revolution and the Making of Soviet Russia, 1917–1921   53

Reading 22	Leon Trotsky Interviewed in the *New York Times*, 1917	54
Reading 23	First Declaration of the Provisional Government, 1917	56
Reading 24	Order No. 1 of the Petrograd Soviet of Workers' and Soldiers' Deputies to the Petrograd District Garrison, 1917	58
Reading 25	V.I. Lenin's "April Theses," 1917	60
Reading 26	Alexander Kerensky as "Persuader-in-Chief," 1917	63
Reading 27	The Decree on Land, 1917	65
Reading 28	"Moscow 1918"	66
Reading 29	Red Terror, 1918	69
Reading 30	Lenin's Address to the Founding Conference of the Communist International, 1919	71
Reading 31	Lenin's Appeal to the Red Army, 1919	73
Reading 32	The *ABC of Communism*, 1919	75

Chapter 5: The New Economic Policy and Stalin's Rise to Power   77

Reading 33	Resolution of the Kronstadt Sailors, 1921	78

Reading 34	Lenin's Announcement of the New Economic Policy, 1921	80
Reading 35	Lenin's "Last Testament," 1922–23	83
Reading 36	Trotsky on the Culture Wars, 1924	85
Reading 37	The NEP Balance Sheet, 1926	88
Reading 38	The Expulsion of Trotsky from the Communist Party, 1927	90

Chapter 6: Soviet Foreign Policy, 1917–1941   93

Reading 39	Decree on Peace, 1917	94
Reading 40	Lenin's Address Urging Acceptance of the Brest-Litovsk Peace Treaty, 1918	96
Reading 41	Left Communists Condemn the Brest-Litovsk Treaty, 1918	98
Reading 42	Thesis on the Condition of Admission to the Communist International, 1918	99
Reading 43	Trotsky and Permanent Revolution, 1906	102
Reading 44	Lenin, "On the Slogan for a United States of Europe," 1915	103
Reading 45	Lenin, "Letter to American Workers," 1918	104
Reading 46	Stalin, "The October Revolution and the Tactics of the Russian Communists," 1924	106
Reading 47	"The Struggle Against Imperialist War and the Tasks of the Communists," 1932	108
Reading 48	Vyacheslav Molotov Radio Announcement of the Soviet Occupation of Eastern Poland, 1939	109
Reading 49	Winston Churchill's Broadcast to the British People, 1939	110
Reading 50	A Propaganda Leaflet Dropped from Soviet Airplanes During the First Days of the Winter War, 1939	111
Reading 51	The Katyn Massacre, 1940	112

Chapter 7: Stalinism as a Way of Life   115

Reading 52	Stalin on the Grain Crisis, 1928	116

Reading 53	Stalin's "On the Liquidation of the Kulaks as a Class," 1929	118
Reading 54	On the Rate of Collectivization and State Assistance for Collective-Farm Construction, 1930	120
Reading 55	Stalin's "Dizzy With Success" Speech, 1930	122
Reading 56	Letter to Stalin and Mikhail Kalinin from Workers at the Red Putilovets Factory, Leningrad, 1930	124
Reading 57	Excerpt from Vasily Grossman, *Everything Flows*, 1970	126
Reading 58	Report of the All-Union Resettlement Committee on Resettling Collective Farmers to Ukraine (with Table), 1933	127
Reading 59	Stalin's Speech at the First All-Union Conference of Stakhanovites, 1935	129
Reading 60	Maxim Gorky's Speech on Soviet Literature (and Socialist Realism), 1934	132
Reading 61	Materials on the Kirov Murder, 1934–1990, Prepared by a TSK KPSS Commission, 1961	134
Reading 62	The Moscow Show Trials, 1936-38	136

Chapter 8: USSR in the Great Patriotic War, Cold War, and Reconstruction — 141

Reading 63	Adolf Hitler's "Directive for the Treatment of Political Commissars" (Commissar Order), 1941	142
Reading 64	Molotov's Radio Broadcast Announcing War with Germany, 1941	143
Reading 65	Testimony of Dina Pronicheva on the Babi Yar Massacre, 1941	145
Reading 66	Stalin's Order #227 by the People's Commissar of the Defense of the USSR, Moscow, 1942	148
Reading 67	Nazi Policies on the Eastern Front, 1943	150
Reading 68	Diary of Valery Sukhov, A Child of Twelve, During the Leningrad Bombardment, 1941	151
Reading 69	Chart of Calorie Allotments for Leningrad Residents During the Siege, 1941	152
Reading 70	Toast to the Russian People at a Reception in Honor of Red Army Commanders Given by the Soviet Government in the Kremlin on Thursday, May 25, 1945	154
Reading 71	Stalin's "Two Camps" Speech, 1946	155

| Reading 72 | Stalin and the Cold War, 1946 | 158 |

Chapter 9: From De-Stalinization to the Brezhnev Doctrine, 1953–1968 — 159

Reading 73	Vladimir Pomerantsev, "On Sincerity in Literature," 1953	160
Reading 74	Cartoon of Khrushchev, the "Kukuruznik," 1956	162
Reading 75	The Warsaw Security Pact, 1955	163
Reading 76	Khrushchev's "Destalinization" Speech, 1956	165
Reading 77	*Pravda* Announces the Soviet Invasion of Hungary, 1956	168
Reading 78	Yuri Gagarin's Parade after Returning from Space, 1961	169
Reading 79	Evgenii Yevtushenko, "Stalin's Heirs," 1962	171
Reading 80	Prime Minister Fidel Castro's Letter to Chairman Khrushchev, 1962	173
Reading 81	Letter from Khrushchev to Castro, 1962	175
Reading 82	The Soviet Invasion of Czechoslovakia, 1968	177
Reading 83	The Brezhnev Doctrine, 1968	179

Chapter 10: Soviet Stagnation and Collapse, 1968–1991 — 181

Reading 84	Economic Stagnation, 1960–1985	182
Reading 85	The Problem of Supply and Demand, 1971	183
Reading 86	The War in Afghanistan, 1979	185
Reading 87	The Decree Against Alcohol, 1985	186
Reading 88	The Chernobyl Disaster, 1986	187
Reading 89	Perestroika, 1988	189
Reading 90	Gorbachev Speaks to the UN, 1988	190
Reading 91	"Assessing the Future of the Soviet Military," 1989	193

Reading 92	The Soviet Economy, 1990	195
Reading 93	The Map of the Commonwealth of Independent States, 1991	197
Reading 94	Boris Yeltsin's "Tank" Speech, August 19, 1991	198
Reading 95	"Yeltsin Disbands Parliament, Calls Elections to 'Federal Assembly,'" 1993	199

Chapter 11: Post-Soviet Russia — 201

Reading 96	"Russia's Economic Transition," 2013	202
Reading 97	Russian Per Capita GDP and Global GDP Growth Rate Since the Fall of the Soviet Union, 1990–2015	203
Reading 98	Male Life Expectancy in Russia and the United States, 2000	204
Reading 99	Russian Parliament Suspends Yeltsin and Swears in Rutskoy, 1993	205
Reading 100	"Troops Enter Chechnya to 'Restore Order,'" 1994	206
Reading 101	Yeltsin's "Resignation" Speech, 1999	208
Reading 102	Election Results: 2000, 2004, 2008	210
Reading 103	Vladimir Putin on the War on Terror, 2004	212
Reading 104	Medvedev and Putin, 2008	215
Reading 105	The Crimean Crisis, 2014	217
Reading 106	NATO Commander Reports on Russian Invasion of Ukraine, 2014	220
Reading 107	Putin Responds to Accusations of Russian Interference in the US 2016 Presidential Election, 2016	221
Reading 108	U.S. Office of National Intelligence Report on Russian Hacking in the 2016 U.S. Presidential Elections, 2017	223

INTRODUCTION

For generations, students of Russian history have studied Thomas Riha's classic primary source collection, *Readings in Russian Civilization*. His three volumes have shaped the experience that thousands of students have had with this important subject (while rumors of his famous disappearance continue). There have been few readers to appear on the market since then. Scholars have turned their attention to important collections dealing with specific subjects in Russian and Soviet history. The Internet has provided a platform for the sharing of vast materials. But perhaps because of the large shadow that Riha's work has cast on the field, few scholars have attempted to compile a new primary source print collection that addresses the significant historiographical shifts that have happened in the field in the last thirty years. Few have worked to uncover, annotate, and synthesize the new sources that have become available since the Soviet Union's collapse.

This collection represents an effort to bring new sources to the canon of primary reading that has shaped students' understanding of Russia's incredible history in the 19th, 20th, and 21st centuries. This collection is new in three critical ways. First, the authors have set out from the beginning to find materials that are not already in common use and that offer unique insights into these critical periods. Poetry, satire, and propaganda posters all have something to say about the world that Russia has inhabited and shaped. Some new translations appear, and the sources reach right up to the present day, dealing with issues like Ukrainian independence and Russian meddling in American elections. The second way that this collection is new appears in the themes that these materials address. While political and foreign policy history still appear, real attention is also paid to large social and economic shifts as well as the ways that culture shapes and moderates people's experiences of their world. Lastly, unlike many primary source readers, the authors have endeavored to keep the readings short and manageable, with thoughtful annotations that provide sufficient context to make these materials understandable to the newest of students. Inasmuch as possible, these readings should be read as though they are in dialogue with each other. Each chapter represents a multifaceted moment when cultural, political, economic, and military events were all happening at the same time and all affecting each other.

The one, immutable law of history is that things happen, and by happening, cause other things to happen, and so on, and on. Everything else is mostly opinion about the meaning or significance of what happened. For instance, in 1917, an array of preceding events enabled the Bolsheviks to seize power in Russia. From the viewpoint of later Soviet history, this was an event of millennial significance for both Russia and humanity at large. From an opposing viewpoint, the establishment of the Communist regime was an historical mistake, even a travesty. Regardless, the Soviet experiment, like everything else in history, proved to be temporary. Its collapse, as its beginning, became just another event in a perpetual cascade of events.

The 74-year history of the Soviet regime is the centerpiece of this new collection of readings on modern Russian history. What we are endeavoring to illuminate through them is not just what the Soviet state was and how it evolved, but also the events and influences that shaped its creation and demise and how that demise has shaped Russia's history since. The various readings are, of necessity, selective. But we have striven for a broad selection that combines official documents with personal memoir and opinion, statistical compilations, and even press accounts. Some are complementary, others contradictory. To provide the selections with some historical context, we have provided each with brief introductions. Collectively, what these readings will hopefully show is that from the late Tsarist era, through the Soviet and into the post-Soviet eras, Russia has always been a dynamic society, full of possibilities and pitfalls and constantly changing. Russian history, like all others, is a journey, not a destination, and this volume of readings is a guidebook.

Many of these readings were written by people who could not speak plainly. They were constrained by the threat of censorship and even imprisonment. They learned how to say one thing and mean another. Many of the readings in this collection will have two or three layers of meaning, depending on the environment in which they were written and who the intended readers were. Often, the annotations accompanying the readings include questions that challenge students to become "Aesopian" readers, like their Russian predecessors. The more that students can hone the craft of reading-in-context, and the more they can see how sometimes words can say many things, the sooner they will begin to think like historians. They will also begin to comprehend the great lessons that Russian history has to teach us all.

chapter ONE

The Great Reforms, Imperial Expansion, and Tsarism under Attack, 1855–1881

READING 1

Landlord and Peasant on the Eve of Emancipation, 1857–1859

The following is a statistical snapshot of the situation in the Russian countryside just prior to emancipation. The most important thing to note is that it was far more complicated than simply landlords and serfs; there were wide variations in both categories.

The Population of the Russian Empire at this time was estimated at 67,000,000. Of this, at least 90% was rural.

SERF POPULATION

- European Russia and Siberia—22,563,086 (There were only 4,338 serfs in Siberia)
- Transcaucasia—506,545
- Total—23,069,631

Thus, serfs represented approximately 35% of the general population and 38% of the rural.

The concentration of serfs was highest in the Gubernia of Kiev where they constituted 58% of the population. In seventeen gubernias and regions, serfs were more than 50%.

Serfs owned by the nobility (dvorianstvo) numbered 21,979,933 or 97.42% of all serfs. The remainder, 583,153 were attached to private factories or government departments.

Dvorianstvo serfs were further divided between landed (or settled) serfs and manor serfs. Landed serfs, the vast majority, were farmers while manor serfs were landless servants involved in various duties or occupations on the estate. In the decades preceding emancipation the number of manor serfs had increased and the number of landed decreased. By 1859, manor serves comprised 7% of the dvorianstvo serf population, or 1,467,378 persons.

At the same time, there were some 700,000 serf owners in the Empire and just over 103,000 serf-holding estates. 3.46% of owners held serfs (0.11%) but no land.

On some 103,000 serf-owning estates:

- 41% had 20 or fewer serfs
- 35% had 21–100
- 20% had 101–500
- .02% had 501–1000

- .01 had over 1000
- 3,800 estates held 43.7% of all male serfs
- Another 20,000 estates held just over 37%
- 79,000 estates (76.7% of the total) held less than 20%

Put another way, 23% of serf owners possessed 80% of male serfs.

Of the above 103,000 estates, 43% were indebted with 7,107,185 serfs pledged as collateral, amounting to 425,503,061 rubles in loans.

Source: A summary of data taken from A.G. Trointsky, *Krepostnoe Naselenie Rossii* (St. Petersburg, 1861).

READING 2

The Edict of Emancipation, 1861

This was the first and the most critical of Alexander II's "Great Reforms." In abolishing serfdom, it addressed a problem long overdue for a remedy, but did it ultimately treat a symptom as opposed to the disease? Pay careful note to the powers left in the hands of the landlords.

Examining the condition of classes and professions comprising the state, WE became convinced that the present state legislation favors the upper and middle classes, defines their obligations, rights, and privileges, but does not equally favor the serfs, so designated because in part from old laws and in part from custom they have been hereditarily subjected to the authority of landowners, who in turn were obligated to provide for their well-being. Rights of nobles have been hitherto very broad and legally ill defined, because they stem from tradition, custom, and the good will of the noblemen. In most cases this has led to the establishment of good patriarchal relations based on the sincere, just concern and benevolence on the part of the nobles, and on affectionate submission on the part of the peasants. Because of the decline of the simplicity of morals, because of in the diversity of relations, because of the weakening of the direct paternal relationship of nobles toward the peasants, and because noble rights fell sometimes into the hands of people exclusively concerned with their personal interests, good relations weakened. The way was opened for an arbitrariness burdensome for the peasants and detrimental to their welfare, causing them to be indifferent to the improvement of their own existence.

WE have begun this task by expressing OUR confidence toward the Russian nobility, which has proven on so many occasions its devotion to the Throne, and its readiness to make sacrifices for the welfare of the country.

WE have left to the nobles themselves, in accordance with their own wishes, the task of preparing proposals for the new organization of peasant life; proposals that would limit their rights over the peasants, and the realization of which would inflict on them [the nobles] some material losses. OUR confidence was justified. Through members of the provincial committees, who were entrusted [with the task] by the corporate organizations of the nobility in each province, after collecting the necessary data, have formulated proposals on a new arrangement for serfs and their relationship with the nobles.

On the basis of the above-mentioned new arrangements, the serfs will receive in time the full rights of free rural inhabitants.

The nobles, while retaining their property rights to all the lands belonging to them, grant the peasants perpetual use of their household plots in return for a specified obligation; and, to assure their livelihood as well as to guarantee fulfillment of their obligations toward the government, [the nobles] grant them a portion of arable land fixed by the said arrangements as well as other property.

While enjoying these land allotments, the peasants are obliged, return, to fulfill obligations to the noblemen fixed by the same arrangements. In this status, which is temporary, the peasants are temporarily bound.

At the same time, they are granted the right to purchase their household plots, and, with the consent of the nobles, they may acquire in full ownership the arable lands and other properties which are allotted them for permanent use. Following such acquisition of full ownership of land, the peasants will be freed from their obligations to the nobles for the land thus purchased and will become free peasant landowners.

A special decree dealing with household serfs will establish a temporary status for them, adapted to their occupations and their needs. At the end of two years from the day of the promulgation of this decree, they shall receive full freedom and some temporary benefits.

In accordance with the fundamental principles of these arrangements, the future organization of peasants and household serfs will be determined, the order of general peasant administration will be established, and the rights given to the peasants and to the household serfs will be spelled out in detail, as will the obligations imposed on them toward the government and the nobles.

WE leave it to the nobles to reach a voluntary understanding with the peasants and to reach agreements on the extent of the land allotment and the obligations stemming from it, observing, at the same time, the established rules to guarantee the inviolability of such agreements.

Towards that end, WE have deemed it advisable:

1. To establish in each province a special Office of Peasant Affairs, which will be entrusted with the affairs of the peasant communes established on the estates of the nobility.
2. To appoint in every district arbiters of the peace to solve all misunderstandings and disputes which may arise from time new arrangements and to organize from these justices district assemblies.
3. To organize Peace Offices on the estates of the nobles, leaving the village communes as they are, and to open cantonal offices in the large villages and unite small village communes under one cantonal office.
4. To formulate, verify, and confirm in each village commune or estate a charter which will specify, on the basis of local conditions, the amount of land allotted to the peasants for permanent use, and the scope of their obligations to the nobleman for the land as well as for other advantages which are granted.
5. To put these charters into practice as they are gradually approved on each estate, and to put them into effect everywhere within two years from the date of publication of this manifesto.
6. Until that time, peasants and household serfs must be obedient towards their nobles, and scrupulously fulfill their former obligations.
7. The nobles will continue to keep order on their estates, with the right of jurisdiction and of police, until the organization of cantons and of cantonal courts.

WE rely upon the common sense of OUR people. When the government advanced the idea of abolishing serfdom, there developed a partial misunderstanding among the unprepared peasants. Some were concerned about freedom and not concerned about obligations. But, generally, the common sense of the nation has not wavered ... .

And now WE confidently expect that the freed serfs, on the eve of a new future which is opening to them, will appreciate and recognize the considerable sacrifices which the nobility has made on their behalf.

They should understand that by acquiring property and greater freedom to dispose of their possessions, they have an obligation to society and to themselves to live up to the letter of the new law by a loyal and judicious use of the rights which are now granted to them. However beneficial a law may be, it cannot make people happy if they do not themselves organize their happiness under protection of the law. Abundance is acquired only through hard work, wise use of strength and resources, strict economy, and above all, through an honest God-fearing life.

The authorities who prepared the new way of life for the peasants and who will be responsible for its inauguration will have to see that this task is accomplished with calmness and regularity, taking advantage of the time allotted, in order not to divert the attention of cultivators away from their agricultural work. Let them zealously work the soil and harvest its fruits so that they will have a full granary of seeds to return to the soil which will be theirs.

Given at St. Petersburg, March 3, the year of Grace 1861, and the seventh of OUR reign. Alexander

Source: Various Authors, *Polnoe sobranie zakonov Russkoi Imperii,* 2nd Series, Vol. 36, No. 36490, New York: Brill, 1990.

READING 3

Emancipation's Aftermath, 1861
The "Long Land Question"

While Alexander II's edict of emancipation abolished hereditary servitude and returned former serfs to their legal status if not as full-fledged human beings, it arguably created as many problems as it solved. The "Land Question" would fester for decades to come and offer no easy solutions.

Under the terms of the emancipation:

- Some 21 million former serfs received collective titles to 116 desiatiny (a desiatin equaled 2.7 acres).

This worked out, on average to 5.5 desiatiny (about 15 acres) per peasant, although actual allotments varied:

- 13% of former serfs received allotments deemed "liberal"
- 45% received "sufficient" allotments
- 42% received "insufficient" allotments

28% of all allotments were regarded as economically unviable, i.e., insufficient to support the inhabitants.

On average, the liberated peasants received 18% less land than they had available as serfs, and frequently land of inferior quality.

Their former masters retained 95 million desiatiny, and almost always the better land.

However, an even more important difference was that the landlords monetarily profited from this partition while their ex-serfs acquired substantial debt. Former serf-owners received interest-bearing bonds from the government in compensation for the land they gave up. The ex-serfs, in contrast, were handed a communal 100% mortgage on the land they received, with 80% owed to the State Bank and 20% to their former landlords. This debt was to paid-off over 49 years via so-called Redemption Payments which were in addition to all other taxes and duties they owed.

Despite this discrepancy, over time the peasants probably came out better than their ex-masters. They were, or had to be, more adaptable and resilient. Thus, by 1905:

- "Liberal" allotments had grown to 34%
- "Sufficient" allotments remained about the same at 42%
- "Insufficient" allotments decreased to 24%

However, largely due to the rapidly increasing population, 52% of allotments were now regarded as inadequate to support the inhabitants. Nevertheless, peasants did not starve because many increasingly found full or temporary work outside agriculture.

Russian agriculture also continued to be burdened by antiquated methods (such as the three field system) resulting in low yields. Even in 1910, Russian grain production per hectare was less than half that of the USA or Germany.

Despite their apparent advantages, the emancipation of 1861 was the death knell of the Russian landed nobility, and their numbers and holdings declined steadily in the decades following. The 95 million desiatiny retained in 1861 fell to 65 million by 1887, 54 million by 1905, and 43 million by 1911. The average size of their holdings also shrank from 790 desiatiny in 1861 to 488 by 1905. Most small and middling estates disappeared; bought up by peasants or the remaining, larger landlords.

Historian G. T. Robinson sums up the result aptly:

> "Whether the general well-being of the peasantry had shown improvement or decline—whether there had been within the mass a tendency to draw together or to draw apart—still, as the day of revolt approached, there was no doubt of the existence in the countryside of a morass of penury sufficiently large, an antithesis between poverty and plenty sufficiently sharp, to give rise to whatever results might legitimately be bred and born of economic misery and economic contrast."

Sources: G. T. Robinson, *Rural Russia under the Old Regime*. Berkeley: Univ. of California Press, 1932; cited in Nicholas V. Riasanovsky, *A History of Russia*. 4th ed. New York: Oxford Univ. Press, 1984.

READING 4

The Table of Ranks (Tabel' o Rangakh), 1722

Peter the Great (1672–1725) created the Table of Ranks in 1722 as a means to compel service from the nobility and to raise new nobles through promotion by merit. It was amended many times thereafter, and by the late nineteenth century, it largely had become a mechanism for building an educated, professional bureaucracy in the civil administration and military. In the 19th century, those attaining the sixth rank in the military/naval lists (colonel/senior captain) and the fourth rank in the civil service (active/senior state councilor) received hereditary nobility. The latter was the case for Lenin's father, Ilya Nikolaevich Ulyanov (1831–1886), the son of a serf, who attained the rank through his service as a state school official. This also made his son, the future leader of the Bolsheviks, a hereditary nobleman.

CIVIL SERVICE RANKS

I. kantsler—chancellor
   deistvitel'nyi tainyi sovetnik—active (senior) privy councilor, first class pervogo klassa
II. deistvitel'nyi tainyi sovetnik—active (senior) privy councilor
III. tainyi sovetnik—privy councilor (from 1724)
IV. deistvitel'nyi statskii sovetnik—active (senior) state councilor
V. statskii sovetnik—state councilor
VI. kollezhskii sovetnik—collegiate councilor
VII. nadvornyi sovetnik—court councilor
VIII. kollezhskii assessor—collegiate assessor
IX. tituliarnyi sovetnik—titular councilor
X. kollezhskii sekretar'—collegiate secretary
XI. korabel'nyi sekretar'—naval secretary (originally naval rank)
XII. gubernskii sekretar'—regional secretary
XIII. provintsial'nyi sekretar'—provincial secretary
   senatskii registrator—senate registrar
   sinodskii registrator—synodal registrar
   kabinetskii registrator—cabinet registrar
XIV. kollezhskii registrator—collegiate registrar

MILITARY (ARMY AND COSSACK) RANKS

I. general-fel'dmarshal—field marshal
II. general-anshef—general-in-chief
III. general-poruchik—lieutenant general
general-leitenant—lieutenant general
IV. general-maior—major general
V. brigadier—brigadier
VI. polkovnik—colonel
VII. podpolkovnik—lieutenant colonel
VIII. prem'er-maior—first major
maior—major
voiskovoi starshina—major (Cossack)
IX. kapitan—captain
rotmistr captain (Cavalry)
esaul captain (Cossack)
X. kapitan-poruchik—lieutenant captain
shtabs-kapitan—staff captain
shtabs-rotmistr—staff captain (Cavalry)
pod' esaul—junior captain (Cossack)
XI. poruchik—lieutenant
XII. sekund-poruchik—second lieutenant
unter-leitenant—sub-lieutenant
podporuchik-sub-lieutenant
XIII. praporshchik—ensign
kornet—cornet (Cavalry)
khorunzhii—ensign (Cossack rank)
XIV. fendrik—guidon bearer

NAVAL RANKS

I. general-admiral—general admiral
II. admiral—admiral
III. vitse-admiral—vice admiral
IV. kontr-admiral—rear admiral
V. kapitan-komandir—commodore
VI. kapitan pervogo ranga—senior captain
VII. kapitan vtorogo ranga—captain
VIII. kapitan tret'ego ranga—junior captain
IX. kapitan-leitenant— lieutenant captain
X. leitenant—lieutenant
XI. korabel'nyi sekretar'—naval secretary (later civil service rank)
XII. michman—midshipman
XIV. michman—warrant officer

READING 5

Sergei Nechayev, 1869
"The Revolutionary Catechism"

In his short life (1847–1882), Sergei Gennadievich Nechayev went from a son of impoverished ex-serfs, to an aspiring teacher, to revolutionary zealot, to dying in a prison cell. His actual career as a revolutionary was largely a bust. His abrasive personality and dishonesty alienated most of the comrades he encountered. Nechayev would achieve lasting fame, or infamy, for the so-called "Catechism of a Revolutionary." Its violent, uncompromising rhetoric would inspire generations of radicals in Russia and around the world, among them, Lenin.

1. The revolutionary is a doomed man. He has no personal interests, no business affairs, no emotions, no attachments, no property, and no name. Everything in him is wholly absorbed in the single thought and the single passion for revolution.
2. The revolutionary knows that in the very depths of his being, not only in words but also in deeds, he has broken all the bonds which tie him to the social order and the civilized world with all its laws, moralities, and customs, and with all its generally accepted conventions. He is their implacable enemy, and if he continues to live with them it is only in order to destroy them more speedily.
3. The revolutionary despises all doctrines and refuses to accept the mundane sciences, leaving them for future generations. He knows only one science: the science of destruction. For this reason, but only for this reason, he will study mechanics, physics, chemistry, and perhaps medicine. But all day and all night he studies the vital science of human beings, their characteristics and circumstances, and all the phenomena of the present social order. The object is perpetually the same: the surest and quickest way of destroying the whole filthy order.
4. The revolutionary despises public opinion. He despises and hates the existing social morality in all its manifestations. For him, morality is everything which contributes to the triumph of the revolution. Immoral

and criminal is everything that stands in its way.

5. The revolutionary is a dedicated man, merciless toward the State and toward the educated classes; and he can expect no mercy from them. Between him and them there exists, declared or concealed, a relentless and irreconcilable war to the death. He must accustom himself to torture.

6. Tyrannical toward himself, he must be tyrannical toward others. All the gentle and enervating sentiments of kinship, love, friendship, gratitude, and even honor, must be suppressed in him and give place to the cold and single-minded passion for revolution. For him, there exists only one pleasure, one consolation, one reward, one satisfaction—the success of the revolution. Night and day he must have but one thought, one aim—merciless destruction. Striving cold-bloodedly and indefatigably toward this end, he must be prepared to destroy himself and to destroy with his own hands everything that stands in the path of the revolution.

7. The nature of the true revolutionary excludes all sentimentality, romanticism, infatuation, and exaltation. All private hatred and revenge must also be excluded. Revolutionary passion, practiced at every moment of the day until it becomes a habit, is to be employed with cold calculation. At all times, and in all places, the revolutionary must obey not his personal impulses, but only those which serve the cause of the revolution.

8. The revolutionary can have no friendship or attachment, except for those who have proved by their actions that they, like him, are dedicated to revolution. The degree of friendship, devotion, and obligation toward such a comrade is determined solely by the degree of his usefulness to the cause of total revolutionary destruction.

9. The new member, having given proof of his loyalty not by words but by deeds, can be received into the society only by the unanimous agreement of all the members.

10. The revolutionary enters the world of the State, of the privileged classes, of the so-called civilization, and he lives in this world only for the purpose of bringing about its speedy and total destruction. He is not a revolutionary if he has any sympathy for this world. *He should not hesitate to destroy any position, any place, or any man in this world.* He must hate everyone and everything in it with an equal hatred. All the worse for him if he has any relations with parents, friends, or lovers; *he is no longer a revolutionary if he is swayed by these relationships.*

11. Aiming at implacable revolution, the revolutionary may and frequently must live within society while pretending to be completely different from what he really is, for he must penetrate everywhere, into all the higher and middle-classes, into the houses of commerce, the churches, and the palaces of the aristocracy, and into the worlds of the bureaucracy and literature and the military, and also into the Third Division and the Winter Palace of the Czar.

12. This filthy social order can be split up into several categories. The first category comprises those who must be condemned to death without delay. Comrades should compile a list of those to be condemned according to the relative gravity of their crimes; and the executions should be carried out according to the prepared order.

13. The Society has no aim other than the complete liberation and happiness of the masses—i.e., of the people who live by manual labor. Convinced that their emancipation and the achievement of this happiness can only come about as a result of an all-destroying popular revolt, the Society will use all its resources

and energy toward increasing and intensifying the evils and miseries of the people until at last their patience is exhausted and they are driven to a general uprising.

14. By a revolution, the Society does not mean an orderly revolt according to the classic western model—a revolt which always stops short of attacking the rights of property and the traditional social systems of so-called civilization and morality. Until now, such a revolution has always limited itself to the overthrow of one political form in order to replace it by another, thereby attempting to bring about a so-called revolutionary state. The only form of revolution beneficial to the people is one which destroys the entire State to the roots and exterminates all the state traditions, institutions, and classes in Russia.

Source: Nechayev, Sergei. *Catechism of the Revolutionist*. New York: AK Press, 1989.

READING 6

Fyodor Dostoevsky, Slavophile Intellectual, 1877

Fyodor Mikhailovich Dostoevsky (1821–1881) is generally recognized as one of Russia's greatest writers. By 1880, novels such as *Crime and Punishment* (1866), *The Brothers Karamazov* (1880), along with an array of short stories and essays, established Dostoevsky as a literary and philosophical influence. After an early flirtation with radicalism, Dostoevsky's views became increasingly conservative and nationalist. He gravitated to the view that Russia had a unique culture with a Manifest Destiny. In the mid-1870s, rebellions erupted among the Balkan Christian subjects (most of them Orthodox Slavs) of the Ottoman Empire. This led to Russian intervention in 1877. This isolated Russia diplomatically and risked a wider war with Britain and other states. In the following excerpts from his personal journal, written in April 1877, Dostoevsky scoffs at Russia's enemies and imagines Russia as the savior of Europe. The deeply religious writer saw Russia's fundamental predicament, and Europe's, not in political terms, but spiritual, and Russia as the key to salvation.

"We need the war for ourselves: we are arising not only for the sake of out brother Slavs harassed by the Turks, but for our own salvation. War will clear the air which we breathe and in which we stifle, sitting as we do in helpless rottenness and spiritual suffocation."

"If society is unhealthy and infected, even so good a thing as prolonged peace, instead of being a benefit to society, becomes harmful. Never has a generation passed in European history, since we can remember it, without a war. And there is a reason: war evidently is necessary for some purpose, is health-giving and eases humanity."

"Perhaps not we, but our children, will see the end of England."

"The fate of Poland awaits France, and will cease to exist politically."

Source: Dostoevsky, Feodor. *Journal of an Author*; cited in E. H. Carr, *Dostoevsky, 1821–1881*. London: Routledge, 2014.

READING 7

Sir Donald Mackenzie Wallace's Observations on Russian Social Classes, 1870s

Sir Donald Mackenzie Wallace (1841–1919) was a Scottish scholar, writer, and, later, a journalist, who lived and traveled in the Russian Empire from 1870–1875, later returning as a correspondent for the *London Times*. His book, *Russia: Its History and Condition to 1877*, details the observations and opinions of an outsider, a Victorian Briton, but it is rich in detail and not without sympathy and insight. Wallace was influential in shaping British and Western views of Russia in the late nineteenth century. Following are excerpts of his observations on Russian social classes and types.

According to Wallace's figures, by the mid-1870s, the Russian Empire had an estimated population of 77,680,293:

- "Rural classes" (largely peasants) accounted for 82%
- "Town classes" were 9%
- "Military classes" (mostly Cossacks) were 6%
- Nobles (hereditary and personal) totaled slightly over 1%
- Clergy, under 1%

"What are social classes in the Russian sense of the term? I may be well, before going any further, to answer this question.

If the question were put to a Russian it is not at all unlikely that he would reply somewhat in this fashion: 'In Russia there are no social classes and there never have been any. That fact constitutes one of the most striking peculiarities of her historical development, and one of the surest foundations of her future greatness. We know nothing, and have never known anything, of those class-distinctions and class-enmities which in Western Europe have often shaken society to its basis, and imperiled its existence in the future.'"

"This statement will not be readily accepted by the traveler who visits Russia with no preconceived ideas and forms opinions from his own observations. To him it seems that class distinctions form one of the most prominent characteristics of Russian society. In a few days he learns to distinguish the various classes by their outward appearance. He easily recognizes the French-speaking nobles in West-European costume; the burly, bearded merchant in black cloth cap and long, shiny double-breasted coat;

the priest with his uncut hair and flowing robes; the peasant with his fair beard and unsavory, greasy sheep-skin. Meeting everywhere those well-marked types, he naturally assumes that Russian society is composed of exclusive castes … ."

"This apparent contradiction is to be explained by the equivocal meaning of the Russian terms Sosloviya and Sostoyaniya which are commonly translated 'social classes.' If by these terms are meant 'castes' in the Oriental sense, then it may be confidently asserted that such do not exist in Russia. Between the nobles, the clergy, the burghers, and the peasants there is no distinction of race and no impassable barriers. The peasant often becomes a merchant, and there are many cases on record of peasants and sons of parish priests becoming nobles."

THE NOBILITY

"The social aristocracy contains many old families, but its real basis is official rank and general culture rather than pedigree or blood. The feudal conceptions of noble birth, good family, and the like have been adopted by some of its members, but do not form one of its conspicuous features. Though habitually practicing a certain exclusiveness, it has none of those characteristics of caste which we find in the German *Adel* [nobility] and is utterly unable to understand such institutions as the *Tafelfaehigkeit*, by which a man who not a pedigree of a certain length is considered unworthy to sit down at a royal table. It takes rather the English aristocracy as its model, and harbors the secret hope of one day obtaining a social and political position similar to that of the nobility and gentry of England."

"There is a very common idea that Russian nobles are as a rule enormously rich. This is a mistake. The majority of them are poor … . The very rich families … are not numerous … . The lavish expenditure in which Russian nobles often indulge indicates too frequently not large fortune, but simply foolish ostentation and reckless improvidence."

TOWNS AND TOWNSMEN

"The genuine Russian towns—and Moscow may still almost be included in their number—have a semi-rustic air, or at least the appearance of those retired suburbs of a large city which are still free of the jurisdiction of the municipal authorities."

"The scarcity of towns in Russia is not less remarkable than their rustic appearance. I use the word here in the popular and not the official sense … . It may be presumed, I suppose that no town is worthy of the name unless it contains at least 10,000 inhabitants. Now, if we apply this test, we shall find that in the whole of European Russia … there are only 127 towns. Of these, only twenty-five contain more than 25,000 and only eleven contain more than 50,000 inhabitants."

"These facts indicate plainly that in Russia, as compared with Western Europe, the urban element in the population is relatively small; and this conclusion is borne out by statistical data. In Russia the urban element composes only a tenth part of the entire population, whereas in Great Britain more than one-half of the inhabitants are dwellers in towns."

"In all these the municipal organization is the same. Leaving out the consideration of those persons who happen to reside in towns but in reality belong to the noblesse, clergy, or the lower ranks of officials, we may say the town population is composed of three groups: the merchants (kuptsi), the burghers in the narrower sense of the term (meshchanyne) and the artisans (tsekhoviye). Those categories are not hereditary castes, like the nobles, the clergy and the peasantry. A noble may become a merchant, or a man may one year be a burgher, the next year an artisan, and the third year a merchant, if he changes his occupation and pays the necessary dues. But the categories form, for the time being, distinct corporations, each possessing a peculiar organization and peculiar privileges and obligations."

"Some idea of the relative numerical strength of these three categories may be obtained from the following figures. In European Russia the merchant class (including wives and children) numbers about 466,000, the burghers about 4,033,000 and the artisans about 260,000."

THE PEASANTS

"Ivan's household was a good example of the Russian peasant family of the old [traditional] type. Previous to the Emancipation of 1861, there were many households of this kind, containing the representatives of three generations. All the members, young and old, lived together in patriarchal fashion under the direction and authority of the Head of Household … . Generally speaking this important position was held by the grandfather, or, if he was dead, by the eldest brother, but this rule was not very strictly observed. If, for instance, the grandfather became infirm, or if the eldest brother was incapacitated by disorderly habits or other cause, the place of authority was taken by some other member—it might be by a woman—who was a good manager and possessed the greatest moral influence."

"The peasant household of the old type is thus a primitive labor association, of which the members have all things in common, and it is not a little remarkable that the peasant conceives it as rather than as a family … . The Head of the Household is not called by any word corresponding to Paterfamilias, but it termed … Khozain, or Administrator—a word that is applied equally to a farmer, a shopkeeper, or the head of an industrial undertaking, and does not at all convey the idea of blood-relationship."

"The predominance of practical economic consideration is likewise conveyed by the way marriages are arranged in these large families. In all respects the Russian peasantry are, as a class, extremely practical and matter-of-fact in their conceptions and habits, and are not at all prone to indulge in sublime, ethereal sentiments of any kind."

"Nearly the whole of the female population, and about one-half of the male inhabitants, are habitually engaged in cultivating the communal land … . The arable part of the land is divided into three large fields, each of which is cut up into long narrow strips. The first field is reserved for the winter grain—that is to say, rye, which forms, in the shape of black bread, the principle food of the peasantry. In the second are raised oats for the horses, and buckwheat, which is largely used for food. The third lies fallow, and is used in summer as pasturage for the cattle."

"The annual life of the peasantry is that of simple husbandmen, inhabiting a country in which the winter is long and severe. The agricultural year begins in April with the melting of the snow … . From the middle of July … until the end of August the peasant may work day and night, and yet he will find that he has barely enough time to get all his work done. In little more than a month he has to reap and sack his grain—rye, oats, and whatever else he may have sown either in spring or in the preceding autumn—and to sow the winter grain for next year."

"Whether the seasons favor him or not, he has at this time a hard task, for he can rarely afford to hire the requisite number of laborers, and generally has the assistance merely of his wife and family; but he can at this season work for a short time at high pressure, for he has the prospect of soon obtaining a good rest and an abundance of food. About the end of September the field labor is finished, and on the 1st day of October the harvest festival begins—a joyous season, during which the parish fetes are commonly celebrated."

Source: Wallace, Donald Mackenzie. *Russia*. London: Cassel, Petter & Galpin, 1877.

chapter TWO

Autocracy Retrenched and the Empire in Flux, 1881–1904

READING 8

Konstantin Pobedonostsev's "Philosophy of Reaction," 1898

Although little remembered today, Konstantin Petrovich Pobedonostsev (1827–1907) may have been the most influential political philosopher in late nineteenth century Russia. As adviser to both Alexander III and Nicholas II, he moved both to reject reform and hold fast to autocracy. The following extracts from his memoirs, published in 1898, offer scathing indictments of democracy and the press.

ON PARLIAMENTARY DEMOCRACY

What is this freedom by which so many minds are agitated, which inspires so many insensate actions, so many wild speeches, which leads the people so often to misfortune? In the democratic sense of the word, freedom is the right of political power, or, to express it otherwise, the right to participate in the government of the State … Forever extending its base, the new Democracy now aspires to universal suffrage—a fatal error, and one of the most remarkable in the history of mankind. By this means, the political power so passionately demanded by Democracy would be shattered into a number of infinitesimal bits, of which each citizen acquires a single one. What will he do with it, then? How will he employ it? In the result it has undoubtedly been shown that in the attainment of this aim Democracy violates its sacred formula of "Freedom indissolubly joined with Equality." It is shown that this apparently equal distribution of "freedom" among all involves the total destruction of equality. Each vote, representing an inconsiderable fragment of power, by itself signifies nothing; an aggregation of votes alone has a relative value … . In a Democracy, the real rulers are the dexterous manipulators of votes, with their henchmen, the mechanics who so skillfully operate the hidden springs which move the puppets in the arena of democratic elections. Men of this kind are ever ready with loud speeches lauding equality; in reality, they rule the people as any despot or military dictator might rule it … The history of mankind bears witness that the most necessary and fruitful reforms—the most durable measures—emanated from the supreme will of statesmen, or from a minority enlightened by lofty ideas and deep knowledge, and that, on the contrary, the extension of the representative principle is accompanied by an abasement of political ideas and the vulgarization of opinions in the mass of the electors … .

By nature, men are divided into two classes—those who tolerate no power above them, and therefore of necessity strive to rule others; and those who by their nature dread the responsibility inseparable from independent action, and who shrink from any resolute exercise of will. These were born for submission, and together constitute a herd which follows the men of will and resolution, who form the minority. Thus the most talented persons submit willingly, and gladly entrust to stronger hands the control of affairs and the moral responsibility for their direction. Instinctively they seek a leader, and become his obedient instruments, inspired by the conviction that he will lead them to victory and, often, to spoil. Thus all the important actions of Parliament are controlled by the leaders of the party, who inspire all decision, who lead in combat, and profit by victory. The public sessions are no more than a spectacle for the mass. Speeches are delivered to sustain the fiction of Parliamentarism, but seldom a speech by itself affects the decision of Parliament in a grave affair. Speechmaking serves for the glory of orators, for the increase of their popularity, and the making of their careers; only on rare occasions does it affect the distribution of votes. Majorities and minorities are usually decided before the session begins. Such is the complicated mechanism of the Parliamentary farce; such is the great political lie which dominates our age … .

ON "FREEDOM OF THE PRESS"

In our age the judgment of others has assumed an organized form, and calls itself Public Opinion. Its organ and representative is the Press. In truth, the importance of the Press is immense, and may be regarded as the most characteristic fact of our time—more characteristic even than our remarkable discoveries and inventions in the realm of technical science. No government, no law, no custom can withstand its destructive activity when, from day to day, through the course of years, the Press repeats and disseminates among the people its condemnations of institutions or of men.

What is the secret of this strength? Certainly not the novelties and sensations with which the newspaper is filled, but its declared policy—the political and philosophical ideas propagated in its articles, selection and classification of its news and rumors, and the peculiar illumination which it casts upon them. The newspaper has usurped the position of judicial observer of the events of the day; it judges not only the actions and words of men, but affects a knowledge of their unexpressed opinions, their pretentions, and their enterprises; it praises and condemns at discretion; it incites some, threatens others; drags to the pillory one, and others exalts as idols to be adored and examples worthy of the emulation of all. In the name of Public Opinion it bestows rewards on some, and punishes others with the severity of excommunication. The question naturally occurs: Who are these representatives of this terrible power, Public Opinion? Whence is derived their right and authority to rule in the name of the community, to demolish existing institutions, and to proclaim new ideals of ethics and legislation?

Such is a current proposition of the newest Liberalism. It is accepted by many in good faith, and there are few who, having troubled to analyze it, have discerned how it is based upon falsehood and self-deception. It conflicts with the first principles of logic, for it is based on the fallacious premise that the opinions of the public and of the Press are identical. To test the validity of this claim, it is only needful to consider the origin of newspapers, and the characters of their makers.

Source: Pobedonostsev, K.P. *Reflections of a Russian Statesman*, trans. R. C. Long. London: Grant Richard & Co., 1898.

READING 9

The "May Laws," 1882

The Russian Empire acquired a substantial Jewish population only with Catherine the Great's annexation of most of the former Kingdom of Poland in the late eighteenth century. The status of Jews under Tsarist rule was precarious from the start but took a decidedly negative turn when Alexander III approved the so-called "Temporary Regulations Regarding the Jews" on May 3/15 1882 (hence, "May Laws"). The Regulations were not temporary and most remained in force until 1917. Between 1882 and 1892, further regulations established Jewish quotas in universities, forced expulsion from large cities, and restricted Jews from voting in local elections. These policies did much to embitter Jews inside and outside of Russia against the Tsarist regime.

1. As a temporary measure, and until a general revision is made of their legal status, it is decreed that the Jews be forbidden to settle anew outside, of towns and boroughs, exceptions being admitted only in the case of existing Jewish agricultural colonies.
2. Temporarily forbidden are the issuing of mortgages and other deeds to Jews, as well as the registration of Jews as lessees of real property situated outside of towns and boroughs; and also the issuing to Jews of powers of attorney to manage and dispose of such real property.
3. Jews are forbidden to transact business on Sundays and on the principal Christian holy days; the existing regulations concerning the closing of places of business belonging to Christians on such days to apply to Jews also.
4. The measures laid down in paragraphs 1, 2, and 3 shall apply only to the governments within the Pale of Jewish Settlement [that is, they shall not apply to the ten governments of Poland]."

Source: Herman Rosenthal, "May Laws," JewishEncyclopedia.com. http://www.jewishencyclopedia.com/articles/10508-may-laws. (Unedited full-text of the 1906 *Jewish Encyclopedia*.)

READING 10

Dostoevsky Praises Russian Imperialism, 1881

During the latter half of the nineteenth century, the Russian Empire steadily extended its control over the vast reaches of Central Asia, a region overwhelmingly Muslim and Turkic. Local emirates became protectorates of the Tsar, and other areas were annexed outright. In early 1881, Russian troops under the command of General Mikhail Skobelev stormed the Turkmen fortress of Goek Tepe (near the present Turkmenistan-Iranian border), which ended organized resistance to Russian rule. The fall of Goek Tepe also resulted in a massacre of between 10,000 and 20,000 persons. For reasons he details below, Dostoevsky saw this lopsided victory as a triumph for civilization, specifically Russian civilization.

Russia is not only in Europe, but also in Asia; the Russian is not only a European but also an Asiatic. Moreover, in Asia, perhaps, we have even greater expectations than Europe. Moreover, in our future destinies, perhaps Asia is the main outlet! ... . In Europe we were hangers-on and slaves, but in Asia we will appear as masters. In Europe we have been Tatars, but in Asia we are Europeans. Our mission, our civilizing mission, in Asia will bribe our spirit and convey us there ... . A New Russia would be created, which would in time regenerate and resurrect the old one.

Source: Mochulsky, Konstantin. *Dostoevsky: His Life and Work.* Princeton: Princeton Univ. Press, 1967.

READING 11

The Measure of Russian "Backwardness," 1880–1890

The Russian Empire was, by far, the largest country in the world in the late nineteenth century, and its vast territory held abundant stores of virtually every natural resource. Its population nearly equaled that of Germany, France, and Britain combined. Yet in terms of economic development, Russia was notably "backward" compared to the West. The following set of statistics from 1880–1890, just prior to Russia's first wave of industrialization, illustrate this vividly.

TOTAL POPULATIONS, 1890 (MILLIONS)

Russia	116.8
Germany	49.2
Britain	37.4
France	38.3
USA	62.6

URBAN POPULATION, 1890 (%)

Russia	3.6
Germany	11.3
Britain	29.9
France	11.7
USA	15.3

IRON PRODUCTION, 1890 (MILLIONS OF TONS)

Russia	0.95
Germany	4.1
Britain	8
France	1.9
USA	9.3

ENERGY CONSUMPTION, 1890 (MILLIONS OF METRIC TONS OF COAL)

Russia	10.9
Germany	71
Britain	145
France	36
USA	147

PER CAPITA INDUSTRIALIZATION, 1880
(BRITAIN IN 1900 = 100)

Russia	10
Germany	25
Britain	87
France	28
USA	38

TOTAL INDUSTRIAL POTENTIAL, 1880
(BRITAIN IN 1900 = 100)

Russia	24.5
Germany	27.4
Britain	73.3
France	25.1
USA	46.9

SHARES OF WORLD MANUFACTURING OUTPUT (%), 1880

Russia	7.6
Germany	8.5
Britain	22.9
France	7.8
USA	14.7

GNP, 1890 (BILLIONS $, 1960)

Russia	21.1
Germany	26.4
Britain	29.4
France	19.7

MILITARY PERSONNEL, 1890

Russia	677,000
Germany	504,000
Britain	420,000
France	542,000
USA	39,000

PER CAPITA GNP, 1890 (BILLIONS $, 1960)

Russia	182
Germany	537
Britain	785
France	515

Source: All figures adapted from Kennedy, Paul. *The Rise and Fall of the Great Powers.* New York: Vintage, 1989.

READING 12

George Kennan on Political Exiles, 1891

George Kennan (1845–1924)—not to be confused with the American diplomat of the same name—was an American businessman, journalist, and writer who traveled in Siberia and other parts of the Russian empire during the 1860s–1880s. He came to view the Tsar's government as a backward, malicious regime and to sympathize with its opponents. The 1891 publication of his *Siberia and the Exile System* stimulated Western support for Russia's dissidents and blackened the reputation of the Tsarist administration. Kennan's account is by no means objective, nor necessarily accurate, but his observations on the character of the exile system and the types inhabiting it are valuable.

The forcible deportation of "politically untrustworthy" citizens by executive order and without trial first became common in the later years of the reign of Alexander II. Administrative banishment had been resorted to, as I have said, before that time as a means of getting rid of obnoxious persons, but in 1878 and 1879, when the struggle between the police and the terrorists grew hot and fierce, exile by administrative process became a common thing, and people who were known to hold liberal opinions, or who were thought to be in sympathy with the revolutionary movement, were sent to Siberia by the score … .

TYPES OF POLITICAL EXILES

1. The Liberals. In this class are included the cool-headed men of moderate opinions, who believe in the gradual extension of the principles of popular self-government; who favor greater freedom of speech and of the press; who strive to restrict the power of bureaucracy; who deprecate the persecution of religious dissenters and of the Jews … .

    So far as I know, it is not pretended by anybody that the Russian liberals are bad men or bad citizens. The Government, it is true, keeps them under strict restraint, prohibits them from making public speeches, drives them out of the universities, forbids them to sit as delegates in provincial assemblies, expels them from St. Petersburg, suppresses the periodicals that they edit, puts them under police surveillance and sends them to Siberia; but, notwithstanding all this, it does not accuse them of criminality, nor even of criminal intent. It merely asserts that they are "politically untrustworthy"; that the "tendency" of their social activity is "pernicious"; or that, from an official point of view, their presence in a particular place is "prejudicial to public tranquility." These vague assertions mean, simply, that the liberals are in the way of the officials, and prevent the latter, to some extent, from doing what they want to do with the bodies, the souls, or the property of the Russian people.

2. The Revolutionists. In this class are comprised the Russian socialists, the so-called "peasantists" [narodniki], "people's-willists" [narodovoltsi], and all reformers who regard the overthrow of the autocracy as a matter of such immediate and vital importance as to justify conspiracy and armed rebellion. They differ from the terrorists chiefly in their unwillingness to adopt the methods of the highwayman and the blood-avenger. If they can see a prospect of organizing a formidable insurrection, and of crushing the autocracy by a series of open blows, fairly delivered, they are ready to attempt it, even at the peril of death on the scaffold; but they do not regard it as wise or honorable to shoot a chief of police from ambush; to wreck an Imperial railroad train; to rob a Government sub-treasury; or to incite peasants to revolt by means of a forged manifesto in the name of the Tsar. The objects which they seek to attain are the same that the liberals have in view, but they would attain them by quicker and more direct methods, and they would carry the work of reform to greater extremes. The socialistic revolutionists, for example, would attempt to bring about a redistribution of the land and a more equitable division of the results of labor, and would probably encourage a further development of the principle of association, as distinguished from competition, which is so marked a feature of Russian economic life.

3. The Terrorists. The only difference between the terrorists and the revolutionists is a difference in methods.

So far as principles and aims are concerned the two classes are identical; but the revolutionists recognize and obey the rules of civilized warfare, while the terrorists resort to any and every measure that they think likely to injure or intimidate their adversaries. A terrorist, in fact, is nothing more than an embittered revolutionist, who has found it impossible to unite and organize the disaffected elements of society in the face of a cloud of spies, an immense body of police, and a standing army; who has been exasperated to the last degree by cruel, unjust, and lawless treatment of himself, his family, or his friends; who has been smitten in the face every time he has opened his lips to explain or expostulate, and who, at last, has been seized with the Berserker madness, and has become, in the words of the St. Petersburg *Golos*, "a wild beast capable of anything."

Source: Kennan, George. *Siberia and the Exile System*. New York: Century, 1891.

READING 13

The 1897 Russian Census, 1897

The General Census of 1897 was the first complete enumeration of the Russian Empire's population ever made. The most obvious thing it reveals is that the Empire was a vast mosaic of peoples, less than half of whom were Russian per se. It also shows that the great majority of the Tsar's subjects were rural inhabitants and that more than four out of five lived in European Russia.

(Numbers are rounded for simplicity.)

TOTAL POPULATION: 125.6 MILLION (UP FROM AN ESTIMATED 78 MILLION IN 1877)

- 86.6% Rural; 13.4% Urban

BY REGION

- 106.4 million (84% in European Russia, excluding Transcaucasia)
- 7.7 million (6%) in Central Asia
- 5.8 million (4%) in Siberia
- 5.7 Million (4%) Transcaucasia

BY ETHNICITY (NATIVE LANGUAGE)

- 84 million (67%) "Russian" Slavs

OF THOSE

- 56 million (44%) "Great Russian" (Russian)
- 22 million (17.5%) "Little Russian" (Ukrainian)
- 6 million (5%) "White Russian" (Belarusan)
- 172,000 Bulgarians
- 13.5 million Turko-Tatars (mostly in Central Asia)
- 8 million Poles
- 5 million Jews (Yiddish speakers)
- 4 million Balts (mostly Estonians, Latvians, Lithuanians)
- 3.5 million Finns

- 2.1 million Georgians
- 1.8 million Germans
- 1.7 million Armenians
- 1.2 million Moldavians (Romanians)
- 1.1 million Dagestanis

BY RELIGION

- 69.4% Orthodox Christian
- 11% Muslim
- 9% Roman Catholic
- 4.2% Jewish
- 2.8% Lutheran
- 1.75% Old Believers (Orthodox schismatics)
- .3% Buddhist

BY SOCIAL CLASS (*SOSLOVIYE*)

- Peasants—78%
- Nobility/Gentry—1.5%
  - Hereditary Nobles—1%
  - Personal Nobles—.5%
- Clergy—1%
- Military (largely Cossacks)—6%
- "Town Classes"—11% (Merchants, Artisans, Bourgeoisie)
- Workers—2.5%

Source: Troinitsky, N.A. (ed.), *Pervaya vseobshchaya perepis' nasleniya Rossiiskoi Imperii 1897*. St. Petersburg: State Press, 1899.

chapter

THREE

The Disintegration of the Imperial Regime, 1905–1917

READING 14

The Manifesto on the Improvement of the State Order, 1905

The following "October Manifesto" was Nicholas II's response to the revolutionary upheaval of 1905. In fact, it was written by Sergei Witte and Alexei Obolensky and only signed by Nicholas with reluctance. Nevertheless, it very likely saved his throne by providing the promise of reform as opposed to reform itself. Carefully compare what the Manifesto offered to what actually was given in the subsequent Fundamental Law.

We, Nicholas II, By the Grace of God Emperor and Autocrat of all Russia, King of Poland, Grand Duke of Finland, etc., proclaim to all Our loyal subjects:

Rioting and disturbances in the capitals [i.e. St. Petersburg and the old capital, Moscow] and in many localities of Our Empire fill Our heart with great and heavy grief. The well-being of the Russian Sovereign is inseparable from the well-being of the nation, and the nation's sorrow is his sorrow. The disturbances that have taken place may cause grave tension in the nation and may threaten the integrity and unity of Our state.

By the great vow of service as tsar We are obliged to use every resource of wisdom and of Our authority to bring a speedy end to unrest that is dangerous to Our state. We have ordered the responsible authorities to take measures to terminate direct manifestations of disorder, lawlessness, and violence and to protect peaceful people who quietly seek to fulfill their duties. To carry out successfully the general measures that we have conceived to restore peace to the life of the state, We believe that it is essential to coordinate activities at the highest level of government.

We require the government dutifully to execute our unshakeable will:

1. To grant to the population the essential foundations of civil freedom, based on the principles of genuine inviolability of the person, freedom of conscience, speech, assembly, and association.

2. Without postponing the scheduled elections to the State Duma, to admit to participation in the Duma (insofar as possible in the short time that remains before it is scheduled to convene) of all those classes of the population that now are completely deprived of voting rights; and to leave the

further development of a general statute on elections to the future legislative order.
3. To establish as an unbreakable rule that no law shall take effect without confirmation by the State Duma and that the elected representatives of the people shall be guaranteed the opportunity to participate in the supervision of the legality of the actions of Our appointed officials.

We summon all loyal sons of Russia to remember their duties toward their country, to assist in terminating the unprecedented unrest now prevailing, and together with Us to make every effort to restore peace and tranquility to Our native land.

Given at Peterhof the 17th of October in the 1905th year of Our Lord and of Our reign the eleventh.

Source: https://en.wikisource.org/wiki/October_Manifesto.

READING 15

The Russian Fundamental Law of April 23, 1906 and the Powers of the Emperor, 1906

Below are the key sections of the Russian Fundamental Law (Constitution) dealing with the powers of the Tsar. They merit close comparison with the promises made in the earlier October Manifesto. Was Russia transformed into a genuine constitutional monarchy or was the Fundamental Law merely the perpetuation of autocracy under the guise of constitutionalism?

CHAPTER I. THE ESSENCE OF THE SUPREME AUTOCRATIC POWER

[...]

4. The All-Russian Emperor possesses the supreme autocratic power. Not only fear and conscience, but God himself, commands obedience to his authority.
5. The person of the Sovereign Emperor is sacred and inviolable.
6. The same supreme autocratic power belongs to the Sovereign Empress, should the order of succession to the throne pass to a female line; her husband, however, is not considered a sovereign; except for the title, he enjoys the same honors and privileges reserved for the spouses of all other sovereigns.
7. The sovereign emperor exercises power in conjunction with the State Council and the State Duma.
8. The sovereign emperor possesses the initiative in all legislative matters. The Fundamental Laws may be subject to revision in the State Council and State Duma only on His initiative. The sovereign emperor ratifies the laws. No law can come into force without his approval ... .
9. The Sovereign Emperor approves laws; and without his approval no legislative measure can become law.
10. The Sovereign Emperor possesses the administrative power in its totality throughout the entire Russian state. On the highest

level of administration his authority is direct; on subordinate levels of administration, in conformity with the law, he determines the degree of authority of subordinate branches and officials who act in his name and in accordance with his orders.

11. As supreme administrator, the Sovereign Emperor, in conformity with the existing laws, issues decrees for the organization and functioning of diverse branches of state administration as well as directives essential for the execution of the laws.
12. The Sovereign Emperor takes charge of all the external relations of the Russian State. He determines the direction of Russia's foreign policy … .
13. The Sovereign Emperor alone declares war, concludes peace, and negotiates treaties with foreign states.
14. The Sovereign Emperor is the Commander-in-Chief of the Russian army and navy.
15. The Sovereign Emperor appoints and dismisses the Chairman, the Council of Ministers, and individual Ministers … .
16. The Sovereign Emperor has the right to coin money and to determine its physical appearance.
17. The Sovereign Emperor appoints and dismisses the Chairman of the Council of Ministers, Ministers, and Chief Administrators of various departments, as well as other officials whose appointment or dismissal has not been determined by law.
18. As supreme administrator the Sovereign Emperor determines the scope of activity of all state officials in accordance with the needs of the state.
19. The Sovereign Emperor grants titles, medals, and other state distinctions as well as property rights. He also determines conditions and procedures for gaining titles, medals, and distinctions.
20. The Sovereign Emperor directly issues decrees and instructions on matters of property that belongs to him as well as on those properties that bear his name and which have traditionally belonged to the ruling Emperor. The latter cannot be bequeathed or divided and are subject to a different form of alienation. These as well as other properties are not subject to a different form of alienation. These as well as other properties are not subject to levy or collection of taxes.
21. As head of the Imperial Household, the Sovereign Emperor, in accordance with Regulations on the Imperial Family, has the right to issue regulations affecting princely properties. He also determines the composition of the personnel of the Ministry of the Imperial Household, its organization and regulation, as well as the procedure of its administration.
22. Justice is administered in the name of the Sovereign Emperor in courts legally constituted, and its execution is also carried out in the name of His Imperial Majesty.
23. The Sovereign Emperor has the right to pardon the accused, to mitigate the sentence, and even to completely forgive transgressions, including the right to terminate court actions against the guilty and to free them from trial and punishment. Stemming from royal mercy, he also has the right to commute the official penalty and to generally pardon all exceptional cases that are not subject to general laws, provided such actions do not infringe upon civil rights or the legally protected interests of others.

Source: Various Authors. *Svod Zakonov Rossiiskoi Imperii*, 3rd series, Vol. 1, Pt. 1. State Press: St. Petersburg, 1912.

READING 16

The Stolypin Reforms, 1906
"A Wager on the Sober and the Strong"

As discussed in the earlier selection on Emancipation's Aftermath, the "land question" continued to vex Russia long after the abolition of serfdom. The needs and ambitions of the peasants were not satisfied, and the landed nobility, the former dominant group in the rural areas, withered away. The Revolution of 1905 vividly displayed the depth of peasant discontent. In 1906, the Tsar's new prime minister, Petr Arkadievich Stolypin, proposed sweeping reforms in the countryside. His primary aim was to break up the traditional commune, or Mir, in which most peasants lived by allowing members, presumably the "sober and strong," to legally separate from the commune and claim their share of the land as a personal holding. The hoped for result would be the creation of a new dominant class of yeoman farmers. The first step was the following decree issued by Nicholas II.

IMPERIAL UKAZ OF 9 NOVEMBER 1906 ON PEASANTS LEAVING THE LAND COMMUNE (*OBSHCHINA*)

By Our Manifesto of 3 November 1905, the levying on the peasantry of redemption (*vykup*) payments for allotment land (*nadel'naia zemlia*) is abolished from 1 January 1907. From this time such lands are exempted from the restrictions placed on them as a result of the redemption debt and peasants receive the right freely to exit the Land Commune and to acquire as individual householders (*domokhoziain*) the rights of personal ownership of holdings from the Land Commune's allocation. We command … that the following rules be established:

- Each householder who has allotment land in communal ownership (*obshchinnoe vladenie*) can at any time ask for his portion of such land to be confirmed as his individual property (*lichnaia sobstvennost'*).
- In Land Communes where there has been no redivision (*peredel*) of the land in the 24 years preceding the application by individual householders to change from

communal to individual ownership, each such householder shall have confirmed as his individual property not only the kitchen garden (*usadebnyi uchastok*), but also all the holdings of communal land in his permanent possession apart from those which he rents … .

- Demands to have areas of communal land registered as individual property (art. 1) are made through its elder (*starosta*) to the Land Commune which is obliged, within a month of receiving the application and by a simple majority vote, to indicate those portions of communal land which are the individual property of the householder … . If the Land Commune does not within this period enact such a decision, then on the request of the householder making such an application, all the steps required will be taken on the spot by the Land Captain (*zemskii nachal'nik*) who resolves all quarrels arising from it and his decision on the subject is final … .
- Each householder who receives portions of communal land … under the present rules has the right at any time to demand that the Land Commune allocate him, in place of these portions, a corresponding portion, if possible in one place.

LABOR INEFFICIENCY

Stolypin's reform rested on the argument that the traditional Mir was grossly inefficient and throttled individual initiative. Justification for this view could be found in the 1897 census. According to this, 93,701,564 persons relied on "agricultural pursuits" for their livelihood. However, of that 93 million only 18,245,287 were regarded as gainfully employed. The remaining 75 million were largely just mouths to feed. Thus, while rural inhabitants constituted 75% of the Empire's population, they were only 55% of the gainfully employed. By contrast, those engaged in "manufacturing and mechanical pursuits," 9.8% of the total population, were more than 15% of the gainfully employed. Likewise, those engaged in "commercial pursuits," 4% of the total population, were nearly 5% of the gainfully employed. Thus, the agricultural sector, along with all its other inefficiencies, appeared to be a huge waste of human capital.

THE MEASURE OF SEPARATION

It was not until the summer of 1910 that the 3rd Duma finally approved all the reforms. The question is what they amounted to. Was Stolypin's reform a success or a failure?

- There were approximately 14,000,000 peasant households, most still containing multiple generations and families.
- Of these approximately 11,000,000 were communal; the remaining 3,000,000 were traditionally independent.
- By 1916, roughly 2,500,000 households had formally separated from a commune, i.e., about 1 in 4 of the households.

In addition:

- 1,500,000 had de facto separated.
- 800,000 had applied for or were ending separation.
- Counting the 3,000,000 already independent, this means that almost 8,000,000 households, or 57%, were actually or potentially independent. Nevertheless, tens of millions of peasants remained in the traditional communal structure.

Growth of peasant cooperatives:

Another arguable indicator of peasant progress was the expansion of cooperative societies.

1901: 2000   1906: 5000   1913: 33,000

PEASANT LAND BANK ACQUISITIONS

Yet another was an increase in land acquisition through the Peasant land bank:

- 1895–1905: 1 million des.
- 1906–1914: 4.5 million des.

MIGRATION TO SIBERIA

Peasant migration to government sponsored "homesteads" in Siberia also saw an increase:

- 1890–1914: 10 million immigrants to Siberia
- 1908–1913: 3 million

Source: Riasanovsky, Nicholas. *A History of Russia*. 4th ed. Oxford: Oxford University Press, 1984. Tsar Nicholas II, "The Stolypin Reforms," Imperial Ukaz of 9 November 1906. Translated by John Slatter. Copyright © by John Slatter.

READING 17

Russian State Duma Elections, 1906–1912

The creation of the Duma (parliament) was the centerpiece of Nicholas II's October Manifesto and the resulting Fundamental Law, and the great hope of reform-minded Russians. Its limitations came as an equally great disappointment. As the following chart shows, the first two, short-lived Dumas were dominated by the Left and Center Parties, making cooperation with the government all but impossible. With Prime Minister Stolypin's electoral "reform" of 1906, balance shifted strongly to the Right. "Left," "Right," etc., are broad categories embracing an array of often antagonistic parties. "Left" also broadly equates to revolutionary socialists of one stripe or another. "Right" included moderate and extremist elements. Distinctions further blurred in 1915 when most of the moderate Right joined the liberal Center in the so-called Progressive Bloc which dominated the Duma with some 240 seats. The "Other" category largely represents national and religious parties, such as those of Muslims and Poles.

	1ST (APRIL-JUNE '06)	2ND (FEB.-JUNE '07)	3RD 1907–12	4TH 1912–17
Left	124	216	33	24
Center	184	99	78	104
Right	45	52	292	284
Other	144	153	26	25

Source: Figures adapted from Walsh, Warren B. "Political Parties in the Russian Dumas." *The Journal of Modern History*, XXII, no. 2 (June 1950): 144-150.

READING 18

Russia on the Eve of Armageddon, 1914

The following tables and numbers give a statistical portrait of Russia on the eve of WWI, after more than two decades of intense and significant economic development. They deserve close comparison with the figures for 1880–1890. One thing that will be readily apparent is that while Russia had narrowed the "backwardness" gap, it still lagged behind the West in almost all key indicators. A critical economic dependency on Germany is also evident. An important, though ultimately unanswerable, question is if Russia was poised on the brink of a great economic "break-out," which was derailed by the coming war and revolution to follow. This much seems clear: economic growth coupled with the Stolypin Reforms had transformed Russia into a dynamic society with an emerging "business elite" of managers, financiers, and stockholders.

TOTAL POPULATIONS, 1913 (MILLIONS)

Russia	175.1
Germany	66.9
Britain	45.6
France	39.7
USA	97.3

URBAN POPULATION, 1913 (%)

Russia	7
Germany	21
Britain	34.6
France	14.8
USA	23.1

STEEL PRODUCTION, 1913 (MILLIONS OF TONS)

Russia	4.8
Germany	17.6
Britain	7.7
France	4.6
USA	31.8

ENERGY CONSUMPTION, 1913 (MILLIONS OF METRIC TONS OF COAL)

Russia	54
Germany	187
Britain	195
France	62.5
USA	541

PER CAPITA INDUSTRIALIZATION, 1913
(BRITAIN IN 1900 = 100)

Russia	20
Germany	85
Britain	115
France	59
USA	126

TOTAL INDUSTRIAL *POTENTIAL*, 1913
(BRITAIN IN 1900 = 100)

Russia	76.6
Germany	137.7
Britain	127.2
France	57.357.3
USA	298.1

SHARES OF WORLD MANUFACTURING OUTPUT (%), 1913

Russia	8.2
Germany	14.8
Britain	13.6
France	6.1
USA	32

NATIONAL AND PER CAPITA INCOME, 1914

	NATIONAL	PER CAPITA
Russia	$7 billion	$41
Germany	$12 billion	$184
Britain	$11 billion	$244
France	$6 billion	$153
USA	$37 billion	$377

MILITARY PERSONNEL, 1914

Russia	1,352,000
Germany	891,000
Britain	532,000
France	910,000
USA	164,000

NATIONAL WEALTH
(TOTAL MONETARY VALUE OF TANGIBLE ASSETS, BILLIONS OF $)

Russia	$60 (1910)
Germany	$83 (1908)
Britain	$67 (1908)
France	$55.4 (1913)
USA	$187 (1912)

1913 PER CAPITA NATIONAL INCOME

Russia	$102
Germany	$300
France	$350
Britain	$460
USA	$700

AVAILABLE INVESTMENT CAPITAL

1900	1.4 billion rubles
1913	4.7 billion rubles

RUSSIAN IMPORTS 1913 (1375 MILLION RUBLES)

Germany	47%
Britain	12%
China	6%
USA	5%
France	4%
Netherlands	1.5%

RUSSIAN EXPORTS 1913 (1520 MILLION RUBLES)

Germany	30%
Britain	18%
Netherlands	12%
France	7%
Italy	5%
USA	1%

Wages were low: the average Russian wage equaled only 40% of the German and 30% of the British. On the other hand, **taxes** also were comparatively low: The Russian tax burden was a third of Germany of France and a quarter of Britain.

77% of the **labor force** remained tied down in agriculture which accounted for only 44% of the value of the economy.

Sources: All figures adapted from Paul Kennedy, *The Rise and Fall of the Great Powers*. New York: Vintage (1989), pp. 171, 199–203, and *The World Almanac and Encyclopedia for 1919*, p. 449, Mark Harrison and Andrei Markovich, "Russia's Home Front, 1914–1917: The Economy" (20 Dec. 2012), https://www2.warwick.ac.uk/fac/soc/economics/staff/mharrison/public/rgwr_postprint.pdf, and M. R. Johnson, *The Third Rome: Holy Russia, Tsarism & Orthodoxy*. Washington, DC: Foundation for Economic Liberty (2003), p. 200.

RUSSIA'S "BUSINESS ELITE"

The value of the Russian stock market doubled between 1900 and 1914. On the eve of the First World War, 2303 joint stock companies dominated its burgeoning capitalist economy. Of these stock companies, 231 were foreign-owned, the remainder, 2072, Russian. The real power rested in the hands of some 1454 directors, managers, bankers, and stockholders who arguably constituted a business elite. This, recall, in an empire with a population fast approaching 180,000,000.

Of these 1450-odd individuals:

- 21% were nobles of one degree or another, including numerous, counts, barons, and princes. A large portion of these also held governmental offices or appointments.
- Another 21% bore the title of Hereditary Honorary Citizen (potomstvenny pochotny grazhdanin), or the less common Personal Honorary Citizen. This was a privileged social rank awarded commoners who had displayed merit in business, the arts, or academic pursuits, and ranked just below nobles and above merchants. Some might call it the party card of the Russian bourgeoisie.
- 8% belonged to the traditional merchant guilds.
- Another 8% held engineering degrees.
- 9% were non-Russians. Germans constituted the largest group followed by French, Belgians, and British. The remainder was Swiss, Dutch, and Austrian.

However, roughly a third were persons of no special distinction beyond the success and influence they had attained in business, including those of peasant background.

Thus, while nobles and honorary citizens were greatly overrepresented among the elite, it was not monolithic and arguably represented a kind of common ground for Russians of different class backgrounds.

Source: Witte, S. and Obolenskii, A. "The Manifesto on the Improvement of the State Order," translated by Daniel Field. 1905. https://en.wikisource.org/wiki/October_Manifesto.

READING 19

Pyotr Durnovo's Memorandum to Tsar Nicholas, 1914

Pyotr Nikolaevich Durnovo (1845–1915) had a long career in Imperial service. He was most closely connected to the ministry of the interior, serving as director of police under Alexander III and briefly (1905–06) as Interior Minister under Nicholas II. Durnovo was extremely skeptical of Russia's alliance with Britain which he believed would drag the Empire into an unnecessary and counterproductive war with Germany. In this and other matters, Durnovo was unnervingly prescient, including his prediction that Russian defeats would unleash the forces of social revolution.

The central factor of the period of world history through which we are now passing is the rivalry between England and Germany. This rivalry must inevitably lead to an armed struggle between them, the issue of which will, in all probability, prove fatal to the vanquished side. The interests of these two powers are far too incompatible, and their simultaneous existence as world powers will sooner or later prove impossible. On the one hand, there is an insular State, whose world importance rests upon its domination of the sea, its world trade, and its innumerable colonies. On the other, there is a powerful continental empire, whose limited territory is insufficient for an increased population. It has therefore openly and candidly declared that its future is on the seas. It has, with fabulous speed, developed an enormous world commerce, built for its protection a formidable navy, and, with its famous trademark, "Made in Germany," created a mortal danger to the industrial and economic prosperity of its rival. Naturally, England cannot yield without a fight, and between her and Germany a struggle for life or death is inevitable.

The armed conflict impending as a result of this rivalry cannot be confined to a duel between England and Germany alone. Their resources are far too unequal, and, at the same time, they are not sufficiently vulnerable to each other. Germany could provoke rebellion in India, in South Africa, and, especially, a dangerous rebellion in Ireland, and paralyze English sea trade by means of privateering and, perhaps, submarine warfare, thereby creating for Great Britain difficulties in her food supply; but, in spite of all the daring of the German military leaders, they would scarcely risk landing in England, unless a fortunate

READING 20

Helphand-Parvus's Plan for Subversion in Russia, 1915

Alexander Lazarevich Helphand (1867–1924), better known by his alias, Parvus, was a veteran Socialist and Marxist theoretician who had worked closely with Trotsky during the Revolution of 1905. In the years following, he moved to the Ottoman Empire where he became involved in commercial affairs and various intrigues. As the following selection details, in early 1915, he approached the German Ambassador in Constantinople, Baron Hans von Wangenheim, with an ambitious plan to remove Russia from the war through revolutionary subversion. As the final note from Berlin's acting foreign secretary, Arthur Zimmermann, indicates, the Germans bit and began to fund Parvus's operation. While Lenin kept his distance from Parvus, other Bolsheviks actively collaborated. In 1917 the Germans, thanks to Parvus, would help Lenin return to Russia and provide his party with large subsidies.

TELEGRAM NO. 76
A 934 BERLIN, 9 JANUARY 1915

The Imperial Ambassador in Constantinople has sent the following telegram under No. 70.

The well-known Russian Socialist and publicist, Dr. Helphand, one of the main leaders of the last Russian Revolution, who was exiled from Russia and has, on several occasions, been expelled from Germany, has for some time been active here as a writer, concerning himself chiefly with questions of Turkish economics. Since the beginning of the war, Parvus's attitude has been definitely pro-German. He is helping Dr. Zimmer in his support of the Ukrainian movement and he also rendered useful services in the founding of Batsarias's newspaper in Bucharest. In a conversation with me, which he had requested through Zimmer, Parvus said that the Russian Democrats could only achieve their aim by the total destruction of Czarism and the division of Russia into smaller states. On the other hand, Germany would not be completely successful if it were not possible to kindle a major revolution in Russia. However, there would still be a danger to Germany from Russia, even after the war, if the Russian Empire were not divided into a number of separate

popular tide, aroused by themselves, and Russia will be flung into hopeless anarchy, the issue of which cannot be foreseen.

February, 1914

P. N. Durnovo

Source: Durnovo, Peter and Frank Alfred Golder (ed and trans). *Documents of Russian History, 1914–1917.* New York: Century Co., 1964.

parts. The interests of the German government were therefore identical with those of the Russian revolutionaries, who were already at work. However, there was as yet a lack of cohesion between the various factions. The Mensheviks had not yet joined forces with the Bolsheviks, who had already gone into action. He saw it as his task to create a unity and to organize the rising on a broad basis. To achieve this, a congress of the leaders would first of all be needed—possibly in Geneva. He was prepared to take the necessary first steps to this end, but would need considerable sums of money for the purpose. He therefore requested an opportunity of presenting his plans in Berlin. He confidently expected an Imperial Circular holding out to the [German] Social Democrats the prospect of an immediate improvement in primary schools and in average working hours, as a reward for their patriotic attitude, to have a considerable effect not only on German Socialists serving in the Army, but also on Russians sharing his own political opinions. Parvus has today travelled via Sofia and Bucharest to Vienna, where he will have discussions with Russian revolutionaries. Dr. Zimmer will arrive in Berlin at the same time as Parvus, and will be available to arrange meetings with him.

In Parvus's opinion, action must be taken quickly, so that the new Russian recruits will arrive at the front already contaminated.

Wangenheim

It would seem advisable for the Foreign Ministry to receive Parvus.

ZIMMERMANN

Source: Zeman, Z.A.B. (ed.) and Dietr Pevsner (trans.). *Germany and the Revolution in Russia, 1915–1918: Documents from the Archives of the German Foreign Ministry*. London: Oxford University Press, 1958.

READING 21

The Impact of WWI on Russia, 1917

The First World War was a human and economic disaster of almost unimaginable scale. For Russia, the war of 1914–17 set off a downward spiral, exacerbated by revolution and civil war which did not end until 1921. The burgeoning economy of 1913 was all but destroyed. In the course of the war, Russia conscripted approximately 8% of its population. Impressive as that may seem, it actually was less than half the percentage conscripted by France and Germany. In large part, this reflected Russia's material inability to effectively arm its manpower. Most of the loans noted below were used to purchase, at a huge premium, weapons and munitions abroad.

HUMAN LOSSES

15,500,000 men mobilized (85% peasants) 1914–17

- 2,250,000 dead and missing
- 3,750,000 wounded
- 3,350,000 POWs

9,350,000 total losses (60% of mobilized)

- 1,500,000 war-related civilian deaths
- 2,000,000–3,000,000 war refugees

TRADE

By 1915: 75% decline in exports; 25% decline in industrial production

Balance of trade: 1913: + 150 MR
 1915: –750 MR
 1917: –1,900 MR

DEBT AND INFLATION

- In 1913 Russian state revenue and expenditure were roughly equal at 3.4 billion rubles

- In 1917 state expenditures were 30 billion rubles; 25 billion were uncovered by revenues
- By 1917 Russia accrued 9 billion rubles in foreign loans plus 8 billion rubles in domestic war bonds (+ 3 BR in pre-war loan debt)
- 40% of Russia gold reserve sent abroad as collateral for loans
- By 1921 the entire pre-war Russian gold reserve will have disappeared
- 1914: 4–5 million rubles printed per day
- 1915: 20–30 million rubles
- 1917: 50–70 million rubles
- From Jan. 1916 to March 1917 consumer prices double
- From March to Nov. 1917 prices triple; prices nearly six times those of 1913
- Jan. 1917: Purchasing power of ruble only 30% of 1914
- Aug. 1917: Purchasing power of ruble 7% of 1914

TOTAL COST OF WAR BY OCT. 1917: 40–50 BILLION RUBLES

- 60% Foreign and domestic loans
- 33% Printing money

Sources: Mark Harrison and Andrei Markovich, "Russia's Home Front, 1914–1917: The Economy" (20 Dec. 2012), https://www2.warwick.ac.uk/fac/soc/economics/staff/mharrison/public/rgwr_postprint.pdf, pp. 7–9, 12, 28; G. F. Krivosheev, *Rossiya i SSSR v voinakh XX veka*. Moscow: Olma (2001), Tables 38 and 52; Steven G. Marks, "War Finance (Russian Empire)," *International Encyclopedia of the First World War* (2017), pp. 4–7, http://encyclopedia.1914-1918-online.net/home/. Edited and compiled by Richard Spence.

chapter FOUR

The Russian Revolution and the Making of Soviet Russia, 1917–1921

READING 22

Leon Trotsky Interviewed in the *New York Times*, 1917

A little known fact is that in the months immediately preceding the collapse of the Tsarist regime, future Bolshevik luminary Leon Trotsky was living in New York. Soon after the Tsar's abdication, the *Times* interviewed him for his opinion on current events. At this juncture, Trotsky was not a Bolshevik. While he expresses the opinion that the new Provisional Government will be short-lived and advocates an end to the war, unlike Lenin, he expressly rejects the notion of Russia making a separate peace with the Germans.

CALLS PEOPLE WAR WEARY.
But Leo Trotsky Says They Do Not Want Separate Peace.

Leo Trotsky, a Russian revolutionist now in America, said last night in the office of the Novy Mir, the Russian Socialist newspaper, that the committee which has taken the place of the deposed Ministry in Russia did not represent the interests or the aims of the revolutionists, that it would probably be short lived, and step down in favor of men who would be more sure to carry forward the democratization of Russia.

Mr. Trotsky said that the cause of the revolution was the unrest of the mass of the people who were tired of war, and that the real object of the revolutionists was to end the war not only in Russia but throughout Europe. He denied that the uprising was in any way a German plot. The revolutionists, even if they had it in their power, would not make a separate peace with Germany. They do not favor Germany, they do not wish to see Germany win," he concluded, " but they are tired of war and the privations of war and they wish to stop fighting."

Source: The *New York Times*, 16 March 1917.

READING 23

First Declaration of the Provisional Government, 1917

In the following Declaration, the new Provisional Government sought to justify the overthrow of the Monarchy, pledged its unswerving support for "sacred alliances" and the continuation of the war, and promised a future Constituent Assembly that would determine Russia's ultimate political course. The prolongation of the war and failure to convene an Assembly quickly would prove the regime's undoing.

FROM THE PROVISIONAL GOVERNMENT

CITIZENS OF RUSSIA

A great event has taken place. By the mighty assault of the Russian people, the old order has been overthrown. A new, free Russia is born. The great revolution crowns long years of struggle.

By the act of October 17, [30] 1905, under the pressure of the awakened popular forces, Russia was promised constitutional liberties. Those promises, however, were not kept. The First State Duma, interpreter of the nation's hopes, was dissolved. The Second Duma suffered the same fate, and the Government, powerless to crush the national will, decided, by the act of June 3, [16] 1907, to deprive the people of a part of those rights of participation in legislative work which had been granted.

In the course of nine long years, there were taken from the people, step by step, all the rights that they had won. Once more the country was plunged into an abyss of arbitrariness and despotism.

All attempts to bring the Government to its senses proved futile, and the titanic world struggle, into which the country was dragged by the enemy, found the Government in a state of moral decay, alienated from the people, indifferent to the fate of our native land, and steeped in the infamy of corruption. Neither the heroic efforts of the army, staggering under the crushing burdens of internal chaos, nor the appeals of the popular representatives, who had united in the face of the national peril, were able to lead the former Emperor and his Government into the path of unity with the people.

And when Russia, owing to the illegal and fatal actions of her rulers, was confronted with gravest disasters, the nation was obliged to take the power into its own hands.

The unanimous revolutionary enthusiasm of the people, fully conscious of the gravity of the moment, and the determination of the State Duma, have created the Provisional Government, which considers it to be its sacred and responsible duty to fulfill the hopes of the nation, and lead the country out onto the bright path of free civic organization.

The Government trusts that the spirit of lofty patriotism, manifested during the struggle of the people against the old regime, will also inspire our valiant soldiers on the field of battle. For its own part, the Government will make every effort to provide our army with everything necessary to bring the war to a victorious end.

The Government will sacredly observe the alliances which bind us to other powers, and will unswervingly carry out the agreements entered into by the Allies. While taking measures to defend the country against the foreign enemy, the Government will, at the same time, consider it to be its primary duty to make possible the expression of the popular will as regards the form of government, and will convoke the Constituent Assembly within the shortest time possible, on the basis of universal, direct, equal, and secret suffrage, also guaranteeing participation in the elections to the gallant defenders of our native land, who are now shedding their blood on the fields of battle.

The Constituent Assembly will issue the fundamental laws, guaranteeing to the country the inalienable rights of justice, equality, and liberty. Conscious of the heavy burden which the country suffers because of the lack of civic rights, which lack stands in the way of its free, creative power at this time of violent national commotion, the Provisional Government deems it necessary, at once, before the convocation of the Constituent Assembly, to provide the country with laws for the safeguarding of civic liberty and equality, in order to enable all citizens freely to apply their spiritual forces to creative work for the benefit of the country. The Government will also undertake the enactment of legal provisions to assure to all citizens, on the basis of universal suffrage, an equal share in the election of local governments.

At this moment of national liberation, the whole country remembers with reverent gratitude those who, in the struggle for their political and religious convictions, fell victims to the vindictive old regime, and the Provisional Government will regard it as its joyful duty to bring back from their exile, with full honors, all those who have suffered for the good of the country.

In fulfilling these tasks, the Provisional Government is animated by the belief that it will thus execute the will of the people, and that the whole nation will support it in its honest efforts to insure the happiness of Russia. This belief inspires it with courage. Only in the common effort of the entire nation and the Provisional Government can it see a pledge of triumph of the new order.

March 19, 1917.

Source: Golder, Frank Alfred (ed and trans). "First Declaration of the Provisional Government, March 20, 1917," *Documents of Russian History, 1914–1917. New York:* The Century Company, 1927.

READING 24

Order No. 1 of the Petrograd Soviet of Workers' and Soldiers' Deputies to the Petrograd District Garrison, 1917

Below is the infamous "Army Order #1," issued by the Petrograd Soviet of Workers' and Soldiers' Deputies and commonly credited with initiating the collapse of discipline on the Russian Army. Perhaps the real questions are why the Soviet, which had no real legal authority, felt it could issue any orders to the military and why the newborn Provisional Government accepted this.

MARCH 1, 1917

To be immediately and fully executed by all men in the Guards, army, artillery and navy and to be made known to the Petrograd workers.

The Soviet of Workers' and Soldiers' Deputies has resolved:

1. In all companies, battalions, regiments, batteries, squadrons and separate services of various military departments and on board naval ships committees shall be immediately elected from among representatives of the rankers of the foregoing units.
2. In all units which have not yet elected their representatives to the Soviet of Workers' Deputies, one representative from each company shall be elected. All representatives, carrying appropriate identity cards, are to arrive at the building of the State Duma by 10 a. m., March 2, 1917.
3. In all their political actions, units are subordinated to the Soviet of Workers' and Soldiers' Deputies and their own committees.
4. All orders issued by the Military Commission of the State Duma shall be carried out, except those which run counter to the orders and decrees issued by the Soviet of Workers' and Soldiers' Deputies.
5. All kinds of weapons, namely rifles, machine-guns, armored cars and so forth, shall be placed at the disposal and under the control of the company and battalion committees and shall by no means be issued to the officers, not even at their insistence.

6. In formation and on duty, soldiers shall strictly observe military discipline; however, off duty and formation, in their political, civic and private life, soldiers shall fully enjoy the rights granted to all citizens.

    In particular, standing to attention and obligatory saluting off duty shall be cancelled.
7. Likewise, officers shall be addressed as Mr. General, Mr. Colonel, etc., instead of Your Excellency, Your Honor, etc.

Rudeness towards soldiers of all ranks and, in particular, addressing them as 'thou' shall be forbidden. Any violation of this rule and all cases of misunderstanding between officers and soldiers shall be reported by the latter to the company committees.

This order shall be read out in all companies, battalions, regiments, ship crews, batteries and other combat and non-combat detachments.

Source: Nenarokov, Albert. *An Illustrated History of the Great October Socialist Revolution: 1917*. Moscow, USSR: Gosizdat, 1988.

READING 25

V.I. Lenin's "April Theses," 1917

Upon returning to Russia (with German assistance) in the spring of 1917, Lenin wasted no time going before the Petrograd Soviet to lay out his plan for taking power. In his "April Theses," Lenin dismissed the Provisional Government as a cabal of imperialist stooges that needed to be replaced with Soviet power. Lenin failed to convince the Soviet leadership of this in April or June or ever, ultimately presenting them with a *fait accompli* in the October Revolution. However, the Theses arguably do demonstrate Lenin's abilities as a master political strategist.

THESES

1. In our attitude towards the war, which under the new [Provisional] government of Lvov and Co. unquestionably remains on Russia's part a predatory imperialist war owing to the capitalist nature of that government, not the slightest concession to "revolutionary defencism" is permissible.

    In view of the undoubted honesty of those broad sections of the mass believers in revolutionary defencism who accept the war only as a necessity, and not as a means of conquest, in view of the fact that they are being deceived by the bourgeoisie, it is necessary with particular thoroughness, persistence and patience to explain their error to them, to explain the inseparable connection existing between capital and the imperialist war, and to prove that without overthrowing capital *it is impossible* to end the war by a truly democratic peace, a peace not imposed by violence.

    The most widespread campaign for this view must be organized in the army at the front.

2. The specific feature of the present situation in Russia is that the country is *passing* from the first stage of the revolution—which, owing to the insufficient class-consciousness and organization of the proletariat, placed power in the hands of the bourgeoisie—to its *second stage*, which must place power

in the hands of the proletariat and the poorest sections of the peasants.

This transition is characterized, on the one hand, by a maximum of legally recognized rights (Russia is *now* the freest of all the belligerent countries in the world); on the other, by the absence of violence towards the masses, and, finally, by their unreasoning trust in the government of capitalists, those worst enemies of peace and socialism.

This peculiar situation demands of us an ability to adapt ourselves to the *special* conditions of Party work among unprecedentedly large masses of proletarians who have just awakened to political life.

3. No support for the Provisional Government; the utter falsity of all its promises should be made clear, particularly of those relating to the renunciation of annexations. Exposure in place of the impermissible, illusion-breeding "demand" that *this* government, a government of capitalists, should *cease* to be an imperialist government.

4. Recognition of the fact that in most of the Soviets of Workers' Deputies our Party is in a minority, so far a small minority, as against a *bloc of all* the petty-bourgeois opportunist elements, from the Popular Socialists and the Socialist-Revolutionaries down to the Organizing Committee (Chkheidze, Tsereteli, etc.), Steklov, etc., etc., who have yielded to the influence of the bourgeoisie and spread that influence among the proletariat.

The masses must be made to see that the Soviets of Workers' Deputies are the *only possible* form of revolutionary government, and that therefore our task is, as long as *this* government yields to the influence of the bourgeoisie, to present a patient, systematic, and persistent explanation of the errors of their tactics, an *explanation* especially adapted to the practical needs of the masses.

As long as we are in the minority we carry on the work of criticizing and exposing errors and at the same time we preach the necessity of transferring the entire state power to the Soviets of Workers' Deputies, so that the people may overcome their mistakes by experience.

5. Not a parliamentary republic—to return to a parliamentary republic from the Soviets of Workers' Deputies would be a retrograde step—but a republic of Soviets of Workers', Agricultural Laborers' and Peasants' Deputies throughout the country, from top to bottom.

6. Abolition of the police, the army and the bureaucracy.[1]

The salaries of all officials, all of whom are elective and displaceable at any time, not to exceed the average wage of a competent worker.

7. The weight of emphasis in the agrarian program to be shifted to the Soviets of Agricultural Laborers' Deputies.

Confiscation of all landed estates.

Nationalization of *all* lands in the country, the land to be disposed of by the local Soviets of Agricultural Laborers' and Peasants' Deputies. The organization of separate Soviets of Deputies of Poor Peasants. The setting up of a model farm on each of the large estates (ranging in size from 100 to 300 dessiatins, according to local and other conditions, and to the decisions of the local bodies) under the control of the Soviets of Agricultural Laborers' Deputies and for the public account.

8. The immediate union of all banks in the country into a single national bank, and the institution of control over it by the Soviet of Workers' Deputies.

9. It is not our *immediate* task to "introduce" socialism, but only to bring social production

---

1 i.e. the standing army to be replaced by the arming of the whole people.—*Lenin*

and the distribution of products at once under the *control* of the Soviets of Workers' Deputies.
10. Party tasks:
    a. Immediate convocation of a Party congress;
    b. Alteration of the Party Program, mainly:
        1. On the question of imperialism and the imperialist war,
        2. On our attitude towards the state and our demand for a "commune state"[2];
        3. Amendment of our out-of-date minimum program;
    c. Change of the Party's name.[3]
11. A new International.

We must take the initiative in creating a revolutionary International, an International against the *social-chauvinists* and against the "Centre".[4]

---

[2] i.e., a state of which the *Paris Commune* was the prototype.—*Lenin*

[3] Instead of "Social-Democracy", whose official leaders *throughout* the world have betrayed socialism and deserted to the bourgeoisie (the "defensists" and the vacillating "Kautskyites"), we must call ourselves the *Communist Party.*—*Lenin*

[4] The "Centre" in the international Social-Democratic movement is the trend which vacillates between the chauvinists (="defensists") and internationalists, i.e., Kautsky and Co. in Germany, Longuet and Co. in France, Chkheidze and Co. in Russia, Turati and Co. in Italy, MacDonald and Co. in Britain, etc.—*Lenin*

Source: Lenin, V.I. *Lenin's Collected Works*. Translated by Isaacs Bernard. New York: Progress Publishers, 1973.

READING 26

Alexander Kerensky as "Persuader-in-Chief," 1917

Alexander Fedorovich Kerensky (1881–1970) was a Socialist lawyer and member of the 4th Duma who rapidly rose from the Provisional Government's first minister of justice, to its minister of war, and, ultimately, to its prime minister and quasi-dictator. Regarding himself a great orator, his detractors mocked him as the "Persuader-in-Chief." His rhetorical skills are in full display in this fateful order for the Army to take the offensive. Although the attack achieved some initial gains, it quickly stalled and degenerated into a full-blown rout. This further depressed the morale of Russian troops, and the debacle was skillfully exploited by Bolshevik propaganda.

Russia, having thrown off the chains of slavery, has firmly resolved to defend, at all costs, its rights, honor, and freedom.

Believing in the brotherhood of mankind, the Russian democracy appealed most earnestly to all the belligerent countries to stop the war and conclude a peace honorable to all. In answer to our fraternal appeal, the enemy has called on us to play the traitor. Austria and Germany have offered us a separate peace and tried to hoodwink us by fraternization, while they threw all their forces against our Allies, with the idea that after destroying them, they would turn on us. Now that he is convinced that Russia is not going to be fooled, the enemy threatens us and is concentrating his forces on our front.

WARRIORS, OUR COUNTRY is IN DANGER! Liberty and revolution are threatened. The time has come for the army to do its duty. Your Commander-in-Chief, beloved through victory, is convinced that each day of delay merely helps the enemy, and that only by an immediate and determined blow can we disrupt his plans. Therefore, in full realization of my great responsibility to the country, and in the name of its free people and its Provisional Government, I call upon the armies, strengthened by the vigor and spirit of the revolution, to take the offensive.

Let not the enemy celebrate prematurely his victory over us! Let all nations know that when we talk of peace, it is not because we are weak! Let all know that liberty has increased our might.

Officers and soldiers! Know that all Russia gives you its blessing on your undertaking, in the name of liberty, the glorious future of the country, and an enduring and honorable peace.

Forward!
KERENSKI,
Minister of War and Navy

Source: Martin McCauley (ed). "Kerensky as 'Persuader in Chief'," in The Russian Revolution & the Soviet State, 1917-1921: Documents. New York: Barnes and Noble, 1975.

READING 27

The Decree on Land, 1917
Passed by the All-Russian Second Congress of Soviets

Lenin penned this brief, initial Soviet pronouncement on the land question which plainly spells out the abolition and confiscation of private property. The details of its implementation were to be derived from a separate, and longer, "Peasant Manifesto on Land" compiled during the summer of 1917. Note that final determination was left to the future Constituent Assembly, a body promptly suppressed by the Bolsheviks in January 1918.

1. Landed proprietorship is abolished forthwith without any compensation.
2. The landed estates, as also all crown, monastery, and church lands, with all their livestock, implements, buildings and everything pertaining thereto, shall be placed at the disposal of the volost [communal] land committees and the uyezd [district] Soviets of Peasants' Deputies pending the convocation of the Constituent Assembly.
3. All damage to confiscated property, which henceforth belongs to the whole people, is proclaimed a grave crime to be punished by the revolutionary courts. The [district] Soviets of Peasants' Deputies shall take all necessary measures to assure the observance of the strictest order during the confiscation of the landed estates, to determine the size of estates, and the particular estates subject to confiscation, to draw up exact inventories of all property confiscated and to protect in the strictest revolutionary way all agricultural enterprises transferred to the people, with all buildings, implements, livestock, stocks of produce, etc.

Source: Marxist Internet Archive, https://www.marxists.org/archive/lenin/works/1917/oct/25-26/26d.htm

READING 28

"Moscow 1918"
The Observations of Arkady Borman

Arkady Alfredovich Borman (1891–1974) was a journalist and son of writer Ariadna Vladimirovna Tyrkova-Williams (1869–1962). Although opposed to the Bolsheviks, in 1918 he found himself recruited as a spets (specialist) to assist trade negotiations in Ukraine. As such, he gained admission to the Kremlin and met Lenin, Trotsky, and other Soviet luminaries. He also acted as a spy for the anti-Bolshevik ("White") movement. Borman's memoirs offer valuable insight into what was going on among the Red leaders in the critical summer of 1918. The first selection deals with Borman's visit to the Kremlin. The second selection records the reactions of the Bolshevik leaders to the mounting crises caused by rebellions and foreign intervention.

"IN THE SOVNARKOM"

Shortly after arriving from Kiev, Vronsky told me that I should make a report to Lenin on the ongoing peace negotiations and on the prospects for trade with Ukraine … . The Kremlin has been turned into a besieged fortress. All the gates, except the Troitsky, were not only closed, but tightly blocked. We're driving in a commissar's car. The first check of the documents is at the bottom of the entrance. It is clear, however, that the guards are illiterate. The documents are not examined, but the look of the car seems to inspire complete confidence. Trotsky is ahead of us in an open car. He acts like a kind of master—confident and calm. The second check at the top under the tower is more thorough. We are in the Kremlin. After the noisy and fashionable streets, the silence and emptiness [of the Kremlin] are striking … . Only the wires of the field phone remind one that in the center of Moscow there are not only inhabitants, but that they are ready for a siege. A large area in front of the building of judicial institutions is filled up with boxes of shells. They are in a mess … . Between them roam prisoners of war in German and Austrian uniforms … . When moving from one floor to another, Latvians stand in the stairwells and check documents … .

We enter an empty room with two or three tables, but without chairs. Several people are sitting on the tables and talking to each other in a half-voice. This is a room in which officials are waiting to be called to the meeting of the Council of People's Commissars … . At the head of the table sat Lenin, next to no one. Behind the wall is Trotsky. On the window ledge, Chicherin reclined … . People's commissars sat at the table.

I knew many of them already in person. Gukovsky, Tomsky, Larin, Nogin, Bukharin, Bronsky. I have never seen Dzerzhinsky [Feliks Dzerzhinsky, head of the Cheka] at the meeting of the Council of People's Commissars.

Lenin is very similar to his numerous portraits exhibited throughout the city. A face of a man who firmly knows what he is doing and what he wants. Sly laughing eyes. Somewhat like a northern merchant. The buyer of calves or a forest clerk. This comparison, I could not shake each time that I met him. Lenin conducts the meeting very confidently. He delivers the summons, asks the opinions of those present, and then, "having heeded the opinion," dictates his decision to the secretary … . Lenin is aware of all the details of management and the relationship between departments. On a particular issue, he asks the opinion of each of the members at the meeting. Their views are divided. Some offer one, others—another. Listening attentively to all those present, Lenin quietly dictates to the secretary [an opinion] completely different from the voiced opinions. No one is surprised by this. Apparently, this is the usual order. With the commissars, Lenin turns unceremoniously, listens, interrupts, and sometimes adds: "Well, you say nonsense." Nobody is offended. The rule of Lenin is recognized by all.

[Lenin] had some power of suggestion over the other leaders of communism. One had to see with what adoration they pronounced the word "Ilich". Yes, it was real adoration. Apparently, you can adore absolute evil … . The Bolsheviks … were just crazy (I'm not saying this as an excuse) … .

MOSCOW IN JULY 1918

I returned to Moscow on the 5th or 6th of July. In […] my absence, the situation has become much more alarming … . The Kremlin was nervous. A real front was forming near Samara. Yaroslavl had been captured by the insurgents. There was information that the Kornilovites (what the Bolsheviks so called all volunteers) were planning an offensive in the south. From all parts of Russia, information came in on the growth of peasant discontent. In Moscow itself … rumors spread about the ferment among the Left Socialist-Revolutionaries, supported by a detachment of Chekists. And then the German ambassador Mirbach was killed. The Bolsheviks felt that enemies were attacking them from all sides and were not at all sure that they would cope with the situation. The most prominent of them have secured secret apartments in case of a coup. In July and early August, Moscow was seething with spontaneous protests against the Bolsheviks. The Cheka still has not started to work on a large scale … . Members of the counterrevolutionary organization walked almost openly around Moscow, and could travel around Russia with legitimate Soviet documents, obtained by persons who had served as Bolsheviks like me … . Arrests took place, but they were either random or of former public and political figures. Some of those arrested were shot in the mass terror, which began in August … . The Russian educated class still could not understand what the Bolsheviks and the Soviet government were capable of. The pace of life changed very slowly. Private stores were still open, and only in July did the last non-Soviet newspaper cease. The general public, at least until July 18th, when the news of the Yekaterinburg crime [the execution of Russian Imperial Family] came, did not feel the anti-Christ nature of Soviet power … .

[During the mutiny of the Left SRs, 6–7 July] the city was quiet and took a siege atmosphere. The main streets were blocked to prevent the movement of armored cars, which the rebels were rumored to have. Latvian patrols roamed the streets and some horsemen rode around ... . All the time it was expected that shelling of the Kremlin would begin. For several hours, the main telegraph was seized [by the rebels] ... . But why did the SRs who raised the revolt do nothing? ... . The rebels surrendered their weapons ... .

The Kremlin did not believe until the last moment that the British would occupy Arkhangelsk [2 Aug. 1918]. The Kremlin was in turmoil ... . On August 2 and 3, at a meeting of the Council of People's Commissars, the situation was discussed. [Mechislav] Bronsky told me that Lenin was very gloomy and did not hide his alarm ... . He stated that in his opinion the position of the Soviet government was hopeless. Yes, this word was uttered by Lenin at the meeting ... . The commissars did not doubt that the English would move on the trains immediately. In a few days they will take Vologda, and in a couple of weeks they may approach Moscow ... . Lenin repeated his arguments, which I had already heard many times from various Bolsheviks, that "whatever happens, it will not prevent the reduction of the number of bourgeois." ... In the city people were seized right and left. Even before the attempt on Lenin [30 Aug.], there were hundreds of prisoners. The commissars, seeing that the British were slow to move to the south, were somewhat cheered ... . It became frightening in Moscow. No one doubted that the Bolsheviks were doomed.

Borman did manage to leave Moscow in August and escaped abroad.

Source: Bortnevsky, Viktor. "Iz zapisok sekretnogo agenta belogvradeitsev v Kremle," *Russkoe proshloe*. Translated by Richard Spence. Kniga 1. St. Peterburg.: Svelen, 1991.

READING 29

Red Terror, 1918

The initiation of "Red Terror" by the Bolshevik regime is commonly said to have been sparked by the attempted assassination of Lenin and the successful assassination of Petrograd Cheka [secret police] boss Moisei Uritsky on August 30, 1918. The call for revenge is loud and clear in selections two and three. However, the first selection, written by Lenin himself and addressed to the comrades of the Penza Soviet, shows that the mass repression of "class enemies" was already underway weeks earlier. Selections 4 and 5 show Zinoviev's and Trotsky's endorsement of terroristic methods. The last selection, from 1919, outlines the brutal methods employed by the Cheka to crush peasant resistance.

1. "Comrades! The kulak uprising in your five districts must be crushed without pity … . You must make example of these people. (1) Hang (I mean hang publicly, so that people see it) at least 100 kulaks, rich bastards, and known bloodsuckers. (2) Publish their names. (3) Seize all their grain. (4) Single out the hostages per my instructions in yesterday's telegram. Do all this so that for miles around people see it all, understand it, tremble, and tell themselves that we are killing the bloodthirsty kulaks and that we will continue to do so … . *Yours, Lenin.* (10 Aug. 1918) P.S. Find tougher people."
—J. Brooks and G. Chernyavskiy, *Lenin and the Making of the Soviet State: A Brief History with Documents.* New York: Bedford/St. Martin's, 2007, 77.

2. "We will turn our hearts into steel, which we will temper in the fire of suffering and the blood of fighters for freedom. We will make our hearts cruel, hard, and immovable, so that no mercy will enter them, and so that they will not quiver at the sight of a sea of enemy blood. We will let loose the floodgates of that sea […] For the blood of Lenin and Uritsky, Zinoviev and Volodarski, let there be floods of the blood of the bourgeois—more blood, as much as possible."
—*Krasnaya Gazeta*, 1 Sept. 1918.

3. "Crush the hydra of counterrevolution with massive terror! ... anyone who dares to spread the slightest rumor against the Soviet regime will be arrested immediately and sent to a concentration camp."
   —"Appeal to the Working Class", *Izvestiya*, September 3, 1918.

4. "To overcome of our enemies we must have our own socialist militarism. We must carry along with us 90 million out of the 100 million of Soviet Russia's population. As for the rest, we have nothing to say to them. They must be annihilated."
   —Grigory Zinoviev, Sept. 1918.

5. "The problem of revolution, as of war, consists in breaking the will of the foe, forcing him to capitulate and to accept the conditions of the conqueror. The will, of course, is a fact of the physical world, but in contradistinction to a meeting, a dispute, or a congress, the revolution carries out its object by means of the employment of material resources—though to a less degree than war. The bourgeoisie itself conquered power by means of revolts, and consolidated it by the civil war. In the peaceful period, it retains power by means of a system of repression. As long as class society, founded on the most deep-rooted antagonisms, continues to exist, repression remains a necessary means of breaking the will of the opposing side."
   —Leon Trotsky, *Terrorism and Communism*, 1920.

6. "*Yaroslavl* Province, 23 June 1919: The uprising of deserters in the Petropavlovskaya volost has been put down. The families of the deserters have been taken as hostages. When we started to shoot one person from each family, the Greens [peasant rebels] began to come out of the woods and surrender. Thirty-four deserters were shot as an example."

   Do not look in the file of incriminating evidence to see whether or not the accused rose up against the Soviets with arms or words. Ask him instead to which class he belongs, what is his background, his education, his profession. These are the questions that will determine the fate of the accused. That is the meaning and essence of the Red Terror.
   —Martin Latsis, Chairman of the All-Ukrainian Cheka, 1919.

Compiled and edited by Richard Spence.

READING 30

Lenin's Address to the Founding Conference of the Communist International, 1919

> Lenin believed that the proletarian revolution in Russia would inevitably lead to world revolution. He did not think Bolshevik power could survive in Russia without it. The March 1919 formation of the Communist International (Comintern) was a bold step to achieve this end. The Soviet state was then beset by enemies on all sides. A Communist bid for power (the Spartacist Uprising) had recently failed in Germany, but in the coming weeks, Soviet republics would spring-up in Bavaria and Hungary. Both would quickly wither, but the Comintern would be a prominent feature of Soviet policy until the 1940s.

Comrades, at the First Congress of the Communist International we did not succeed in getting representatives from all countries where this organization has most faithful friends and where there are workers whose sympathies are entirely with us. Allow me, therefore, to begin with a short quotation which will show you that in reality we have more friends than we can see, than we know and than we were able to assemble here, in Moscow, despite all persecution, despite the entire, seemingly omnipotent, union of the bourgeoisie of the whole world. This persecution has gone to such lengths as to attempt to surround us with a sort of Great Wall of China, and to deport Bolsheviks in dozens from the freest republics of the world. They seem to be scared stiff that ten or a dozen Bolsheviks will infect the whole world. But we, of course, know that this fear is ridiculous—because they have already infected the whole world, because the Russian workers' struggle has already convinced working people everywhere that the destiny of the world revolution is being decided here, in Russia.

The Soviet movement, comrades, is the form which has been won in Russia, which is now spreading throughout the world and the very name of which gives the workers a complete program. I hope that we, having had the good fortune to develop the Soviet form to victory, will not become swelled-headed about it.

We know very well that the reason we were the first to take part in a Soviet proletarian revolution was not because we were as well or better prepared than other workers, but because we were worse prepared. This is why we were faced with the most savage and decrepit enemy, and it is this that accounted for the outward scale of the revolution.

But we also know that the Soviets exist here to this day, that they are grappling with gigantic difficulties which originate from an inadequate cultural level and from the burden that has weighed down on us for more than a year, on us who stand alone at our posts, at a time when we are surrounded on all sides by enemies, and when, as you know perfectly well, harrowing ordeals, the hardships of famine and terrible suffering have befallen us.

And this First Congress of the Communist International, which has made the point that throughout the world the Soviets are winning the sympathy of the workers, shows us that the victory of the world communist revolution is assured. The bourgeoisie will continue to vent their fury in a number of countries; the bourgeoisie there are just beginning to prepare the destruction of the best people, the best representatives of socialism, as is evident from the brutal murder of Rosa Luxemburg and Karl Liebknecht by the white guards. These sacrifices are inevitable. We seek no agreement with the bourgeoisie, we are marching to the final and decisive battle against them. But we know that after the ordeal, agony and distress of the war, when the people throughout the world are fighting for demobilization, when they feel they have been betrayed and appreciate how incredibly heavy the burden of taxation is that has been placed upon them by the capitalists who killed tens of millions of people to decide who would receive more of the profits—we know that these brigands' rule is at an end!

Now that the meaning of the word "Soviet" is understood by everybody, the victory of the communist revolution is assured. The comrades present in this hall saw the founding of the first Soviet republic; now they see the founding of the Third, Communist International (applause), and they will all see the founding of the World Federative Republic of Soviets. (Applause.)

Source: Lenin, V.I. *Collected Works*, Vol. 28, 4th English Edition. Moscow: Progress Publishers, 1972.

READING 31

Lenin's Appeal to the Red Army, 1919

The following originated as a radio pep-talk delivered by Lenin to embattled Red Army forces in the spring of 1919. At that time, the Russian Civil War was in full swing, and a Red victory still a doubtful proposition. White forces under Admiral Kolchak were pushing to the Volga from the east, while Cossacks and the Volunteer Army of Gen. Denikin were gathering for a drive on Moscow from the south. Still other White armies were active in the Baltic States and the far north. All, as Lenin notes, received material and financial support from the Western powers.

Comrades, Red Army men! The capitalists of Britain, America and France are waging war against Russia. They are taking revenge on the Soviet workers' and peasants' republic for having overthrown the power of the landowners and capitalists and thereby set an example to all the nations of the globe. The capitalists of Britain, France and America are helping with money and munitions the Russian landowners who are bringing troops from Siberia, the Don and North Caucasus against Soviet power for the purpose of restoring the rule of the tsar and the power of the landowners and capitalists. But this will not happen. The Red Army has closed its ranks, has risen up and driven the landowners' troops and whiteguard officers from the Volga, has recaptured Riga and almost the whole of the Ukraine, and is marching towards Odessa and Rostov. A little more effort, a few more months of fighting the enemy, and victory will be ours. The Red Army is strong because it is consciously and unitedly marching into battle for the peasants' land, for the rule of the workers and peasants, for Soviet power.

The Red Army is invincible because it has united millions of working peasants with the workers who have now learned to fight, have acquired comradely discipline, who do not lose heart, who become steeled after slight reverses, and are more and more boldly marching against the enemy, convinced he will soon be defeated.

Comrades, Red Army men! The alliance of the workers and peasants of the Red Army is firm, close and insoluble. The kulaks, the very rich peasants, are trying to foment revolts against Soviet power, but they constitute an insignificant minority. They rarely succeed in fooling the peasants, and then not for long. The peasants know that only in alliance with the workers can they vanquish the landowners. Sometimes, in the rural districts people call themselves Communists who are actually the worst enemies of the working people, bullies who hang on to the authorities in pursuit of their own selfish aims, and who resort to deception, commit acts of injustice and wrong the middle peasant. The workers' and peasants' government has firmly decided to fight against these people and clear them out of the countryside. The middle peasants are not enemies but friends of the workers, friends of Soviet power. The class-conscious workers and genuine Soviet people treat the middle peasants as comrades. The middle peasants do not exploit the labor of others, they do not grow rich at other people's expense, as the kulaks do; the middle peasants work themselves, they live by their own labor. The Soviet government will crush the kulaks, will comb out of the villages those who treat the middle peasants unjustly and, come what may, will pursue the policy of alliance between the workers and all the working peasants-both poor and middle peasants.

This alliance is growing all over the world. The revolution is drawing nigh, it is everywhere maturing. A few days ago it was victorious in Hungary. In Hungary, Soviet power, workers' government, has been established. This is what all nations will inevitably do.

Comrades, Red Army men! Be staunch, firm and united. March boldly forward against the enemy. Victory will be ours. The power of the landowners and the capitalists, broken in Russia, will be defeated throughout the world.

March 29

Source: Lenin, V.I. *Collected Works*, Vol. 29, 4th English Edition. Moscow: Progress Publishers, 1972.

READING 32

The *ABC of Communism*, 1919

Written during the Russian Civil War, the *ABC of Communism* (Azbuka Kommunizma) aimed to explain what the Bolshevik regime stood for and rally workers and peasants to the Soviet cause. It subsequently became a basic textbook of Communist doctrine both inside and outside the USSR as this English translation illustrates. The authors, Bukharin and Preobrazhensky, would both perish in Stalin's purges.

"CHARACTERISTICS OF THE COMMUNIST SYSTEM"

It is evident that the new society must be much more solidly constructed than capitalism. As soon as the fundamental contradictions of capitalism have destroyed the capitalist system, upon the ruins of that system there must arise a new society which will be free from the contradictions of the old. That is to say, the communist method of production must present the following characteristics: In the first place it must be an organized society; it must be free from anarchy of production, from competition between individual entrepreneurs, from wars and crises. In the second place it must be a *classless* society, not a society in which the two halves are at eternal enmity one with the other; it must not be a society in which one class exploits the other. Now a society in which there are no classes, and in which production is organized, can only be a society of comrades, a *communist society based upon labor*.

Let us examine this society more closely.

The basis of communist society must be the social ownership of the means of production and exchange. Machinery, locomotives, steamships, factory buildings, warehouses, grain elevators, mines, telegraphs and telephones, the land, sheep, horses, and cattle, must all be at the disposal of society. All these means of production must be under the control of society as a whole, and not as at present under the control of individual capitalists or capitalist combines. What do we mean by 'society as a whole'? We mean that ownership and control is not the privilege of a class but of all the persons who make up society. In these circumstances society will be transformed into a huge working organization for cooperative production. There will then be neither disintegration of production nor anarchy of production. In such a social order, production will be organized. No longer will one enterprise compete with another; the factories, workshops, mines, and other productive institutions will all be subdivisions, as it were, of one vast people's workshop, which will embrace the entire national economy of production. It is obvious that so comprehensive an organization presupposes a general plan of production. If all the factories and workshops together with the whole of agricultural production are combined to form an immense cooperative enterprise, it is obvious that everything must be precisely calculated. We must know in advance how much labor to assign to the various branches of industry; what products are required and how much of each it is necessary to produce; how and where machines must be provided. These and similar details must be thought out beforehand, with approximate accuracy at least; and the work must be guided in conformity with our calculations. This is how the organization of communist production will be effected. Without a general plan, without a general directive system, and without careful calculation and book-keeping, there can be no organization. But in the communist social order, there is such a plan.

The cooperative character of communist production is likewise displayed in every detail of organization. Under communism, for example, there will not be permanent managers of factories, nor will there be persons who do one and the same kind of work throughout their lives. Under capitalism, if a man is a bootmaker, he spends his whole life in making boots (the cobbler sticks to his last); if he is a pastrycook, he spends all his life baking cakes; if he is the manager of a factory, he spends his days in issuing orders and in administrative work; if he is a mere laborer, his whole life is spent in obeying orders. Nothing of this sort happens in communist society. Under communism people receive a many-sided culture, and find themselves at home in various branches of production: today I work in an administrative capacity, I reckon up how many felt boots or how many French rolls must be produced in the following month; tomorrow I shall be working in a soapfactory, next month perhaps in a steam-laundry, and the month after in an electric power station. This will be possible when all the members of society have been suitably educated.

Source: Bukharin, Nikolai and Yevgeny Preobrazhensky. *The ABC of Communism*. New York: Penguin Books, 1969.

chapter FIVE

The New Economic Policy and Stalin's Rise to Power

READING 33

Resolution of the Kronstadt Sailors, 1921

In early 1921, growing unrest against Communist rule, especially among the peasants, erupted in armed rebellions. While the uprising of sailors and soldiers at the Kronstadt naval base was not the largest of these revolts, it was the most visible and dangerous because of its proximity to Petrograd. Days before the protest flared into open fighting, the Kronstadt sailors approved a list of demands. The Communists later presented the Kronstadt rebellion as a counter-revolutionary adventure linked to the White Guards. The following resolution argues this was not an accurate portrayal. Many of the demands of the sailors later were echoed in Lenin's New Economic Policy.

RESOLUTION OF THE GENERAL MEETING OF THE CREWS OF THE FIRST AND SECOND SQUADRONS OF THE BALTIC FLEET, MARCH I, 1921

1. In view of the fact that the present Soviets do not express the will of the workers and peasants, immediately to hold new elections by secret ballot, the pre-election campaign to have full freedom of agitation among the workers and peasants;
2. To establish freedom of speech and press for workers and peasants, for Anarchists and left Socialist parties;
3. To secure freedom of assembly for labor unions and peasant Organizations.
4. To call a nonpartisan Conference of the workers, Red Army soldiers and sailors of Petrograd, Kronstadt, and of Petrograd Province, no later than March 10, 1921;
5. To liberate all political prisoners of Socialist parties, as well as all workers, peasants, soldiers, and sailors imprisoned in connection with the labor and peasant movements;

6. To elect a Commission to review the cases of those held in prisons and concentration camps;
7. To abolish all [political bureaus] because no party should be given special privileges in the propagation of its ideas or receive the financial support of the Government for such purposes. Instead there should be established educational and cultural commissions, locally elected and financed by the Government;
8. To abolish immediately all zagryaditelniye otryadi [armed requisitioning detachments];
9. To equalize the rations of all who work, with the exception of those employed in trades detrimental to health;
10. To abolish the Communist fighting detachments in all branches of the Army, as well as the Communist guards kept on duty in mills and factories. Should such guards or military detachments be found necessary, they are to be appointed in the army from the ranks, and in the factories according to the judgment of the workers;
11. To give the peasants full freedom of action in regard to their land, and also the right to keep cattle, on condition that the peasants manage with their own means; that is, without employing hired labor;
12. To request all branches of the Army, as well as our comrades the military kursanty [Red officer cadets], to concur in our resolutions;
13. To demand that the press give the fullest publicity to our resolutions;
14. To appoint a Travelling Commission of Control;
15. To permit free kustarnoye [individual small scale] production by one's own efforts.

Source: Berkman, Alexander. *The Kronstadt Rebellion*. London: Der Syndicalist, 1922.

READING 34

Lenin's Announcement of the New Economic Policy, 1921
"Tax In Kind, Freedom To Trade, And Concessions"

In the spring of 1921, spurred by a wave of peasant rebellions and the general collapse of the economy, Lenin abruptly proclaimed an end to the draconian policies of War Communism. In its place, he offered the New Economic Policy (NEP) which would endure for most of the 1920s. In essence, the NEP restored Capitalist incentives in agriculture, retail trade, and foreign concessions. In the excerpts below, Lenin explains and justifies this change which encountered much opposition in the Party.

The Civil War of 1918-20 aggravated the havoc in the country, retarded the restoration of its productive forces, and bled the proletariat more than any other class. To this was added the 1920 crop failure, the fodder shortage and the loss of cattle, which still further retarded the rehabilitation of transport and industry, because, among other things, it interfered with the employment of peasants' horses for carting wood, our main type of fuel.

As a result, the political situation in the spring of 1921 was such that immediate, very resolute and urgent measures had to be taken to improve the condition of the peasants and to increase their productive forces.

Thus, the first thing we need is immediate and serious measures to raise the productive forces of the peasantry.

This cannot be done without making important changes in our food policy. One such change was the replacement of the surplus appropriation system by the tax in kind, which implies a free market, at least in local economic exchange, after the tax has been paid.

What is the essence of this change?

The tax in kind is one of the forms of transition from that peculiar War Communism, which was forced on us by extreme want, ruin and war, to regular socialist exchange of products. The latter, in its turn, is one of the forms of transition from socialism, with the peculiar features due to the predominantly small-peasant population, to communism.

Under this peculiar War Communism we actually took from the peasant all his surpluses—and sometimes even a part of his necessaries—to meet the requirements of the army and sustain the workers. Most of it we took on loan, for paper money. But for that, we would not have beaten the landowners and capitalists in a ruined small-peasant country. The fact that we did (in spite of the help our exploiters got from the most powerful countries of the world) shows not only the miracles of heroism the workers and peasants can perform in the struggle for their emancipation; it also shows that when the Mensheviks, Socialist-Revolutionaries and Kautsky and Co. *blamed* us for this War Communism they were acting as lackeys of the bourgeoisie. We deserve credit for it.

The tax in kind is a transition to this policy. We are still so ruined and crushed by the burden of war (which was on but yesterday and could break out anew tomorrow, owing to the rapacity and malice of the capitalists) that we cannot give the peasant manufactured goods in return for *all* the grain we need. Being aware of this, we are introducing the tax in kind, that is, we shall take the minimum of grain we require (for the army and the workers) in the form of a tax and obtain the rest in exchange for manufactured goods.

There is something else we must not forget. Our poverty and ruin are so great that we cannot restore large-scale socialist state industry *at one stroke*. This can be done with large stocks of grain and fuel in the big industrial centers, replacement of worn-out machinery, and so on. Experience has convinced us that this cannot be done at one stroke, and we know that after the ruinous imperialist war even the wealthiest and most advanced countries will be able to solve this problem only over a fairly long period of years. Hence, it is necessary, to a certain extent, to help to restore *small* industry, which does not demand of the state machines, large stocks of raw material, fuel and food, and which can immediately render some assistance to peasant farming and increase its productive forces right away.

What is to be the effect of all this?

It is the revival of the petty bourgeoisie and of capitalism on the basis of some freedom of trade (if only local). That much is certain and it is ridiculous to shut our eyes to it.

Is it necessary? Can it be justified? Is it not dangerous?

Many such questions are being asked, and most are merely evidence of simple-mindedness, to put it mildly.

What is the policy the socialist proletariat can pursue in the face of this economic reality? Is it to give the small peasant *all* he needs of the goods produced by large-scale socialist industries in exchange for his grain and raw materials? This would be the most desirable and "correct" policy—and we have started on it. But we cannot supply *all* the goods, very far from it; nor shall we be able to do so very soon—at all events not until we complete the first stage of the electrification of the whole country.

Can the Soviet state and the dictatorship of the proletariat be combined with state capitalism? Are they compatible?

Of course they are. This is exactly what I argued in May 1918. I hope I had proved it then. I had also proved that state capitalism is a step forward compared with the small proprietor (both small-patriarchal and petty-bourgeois) element. Those who compare state capitalism only with socialism commit a host of mistakes, for in the present political and economic circumstances it is essential to compare state capitalism also with petty-bourgeois production.

In order to approach the solution of this problem we must first of all picture to ourselves as distinctly as possible what state capitalism will and can be in practice inside the Soviet system and within the framework of the Soviet state.

Concessions are the simplest example of how the Soviet government directs the development of capitalism into the channels of state capitalism and "implants" state capitalism. We all agree now that concessions are necessary, but have we all thought about the implications? What are concessions under the Soviet system, viewed in the light of the above-mentioned forms of economy and their interrelations? They are an agreement, an alliance, a bloc between the Soviet, i.e., proletarian, state power and state capitalism against the small-proprietor (patriarchal and petty-bourgeois) element. The concessionaire is a capitalist. He conducts his business on capitalist lines, for profit, and is willing to enter into an agreement with the proletarian government in order to obtain super-profits or raw materials which he cannot otherwise obtain, or can obtain only with great difficulty. Soviet power gains by the development of the productive forces, and by securing an increased quantity of goods immediately, or within a very short period. We have, say, a hundred oilfields, mines and forest tracts.

The most important task that confronts all Party and Soviet workers in connection with the introduction of the tax in kind is to apply the principles of the "concessions" policy (i.e., a policy that is similar to "concession" state capitalism) to the other forms of capitalism—unrestricted trade, local exchange, etc.

April 21, 1921

Source: Lenin, V.I. *Collected Works*, 1st English Edition, Vol. 32. Translated by Jim Riordan. Moscow: Progress Publishers, 1968.

READING 35

Lenin's "Last Testament," 1922–23

Lenin wrote the following during the close of 1922 and the beginning of 1923. Whether he realized it or not, he was a dying man. He had already suffered two debilitating strokes and a third, in May 1923, would leave him without the ability to speak. Despite his wish to have his views known to the Party, his wife, Nadezhda Krupskaya, kept the Testament secret until after Lenin's death in January 1924. It is as close as Lenin ever came to naming a successor but, in fact, he does not. While the Testament is most notable for its criticism of the newly-appointed Party secretary, Joseph Stalin, it finds no one without faults.

Comrade Stalin, having become Secretary-General, has unlimited authority concentrated in his hands, and I am not sure whether he will always be capable of using that authority with sufficient caution. Comrade Trotsky, on the other hand, as his struggle against the C.C. on the question of the People's Commissariat of Communications has already proved, is distinguished not only by outstanding ability. He is personally perhaps the most capable man in the present C.C., but he has displayed excessive self-assurance and shown excessive preoccupation with the purely administrative side of the work.

These two qualities of the two outstanding leaders of the present C.C. can inadvertently lead to a split, and if our Party does not take steps to avert this, the split may come unexpectedly.

Stalin is too coarse and this defect, although quite tolerable in our midst and in dealing among us Communists, becomes intolerable in a Secretary-General. That is why I suggest that the comrades think about a way of removing Stalin from that post and appointing another man in his stead who in all other respects differs from Comrade Stalin in having only one advantage, namely, that of being more tolerant, more loyal, more polite and more considerate to the comrades, less capricious, etc. This circumstance may appear to be a negligible detail. But I think that from the standpoint of safeguards against a split and from the standpoint of what I wrote above about the relationship between Stalin and Trotsky it is not a [minor] detail, but it is a detail which can assume decisive importance.

The October episode with Zinoviev and Kamenev [their opposition to seizing power in October 1917] was, of course, no accident, but neither can the blame for it be laid upon them personally, any more than non-Bolshevism can upon Trotsky.

[Bukharin and Pyatakov] are, in my opinion, the most outstanding figures (among the younger ones), and the following must be borne in mind about them: Bukharin is not only a most valuable and major theorist of the Party; he is also rightly considered the favorite of the whole Party, but his theoretical views can be classified as fully Marxist only with the great reserve, for there is something scholastic about him (he has never made a study of dialectics, and, I think, never fully appreciated it).

As for Pyatakov, he is unquestionably a man of outstanding will and outstanding ability, but shows far too much zeal for administrating and the administrative side of the work to be relied upon in a serious political matter.

Both of these remarks, of course, are made only for the present, on the assumption that both these outstanding and devoted Party workers fail to find an occasion to enhance their knowledge and amend their one-sidedness.

Source: Lenin, V.I. *Collected Works*, 4th English Edition, Vol. 36. Translated by Jim Riordan. Moscow: Progress Publishers, 1972.

READING 36

Trotsky on the Culture Wars, 1924
"Proletarian Culture and Proletarian Art"

The following are excerpts from Trotsky's foray into the Soviet "Culture Wars" of the 1920s. Like most of Trotsky's writings, they were suppressed under Stalin. However, in 1924, Trotsky was still at or near the peak of his power in the Soviet hierarchy, and his words carried weight. The basic question was whether and how a distinct "Proletarian" culture could be created. Trotsky's basic answer was that the Soviet regime and the Revolution had more important things to worry about.

Every ruling class creates its own culture, and consequently, its own art. History has known the slave-owning cultures of the East and of classic antiquity, the feudal Culture of mediaeval Europe and the bourgeois culture which now rules the world. It would follow from this, that the proletariat has also to create its own culture and its own art.

The formless talk about proletarian culture, in antithesis to bourgeois culture, feeds on the extremely uncritical identification of the historic destinies of the proletariat with those of the bourgeoisie. A shallow and purely liberal method of making analogies of historic forms has nothing in common with Marxism. There is no real analogy between the historic development of the bourgeoisie and of the working-class.

Our task in Russia is complicated by the poverty of our entire Cultural tradition and by the material destruction wrought by the events of the last decade. After the conquest of power and after almost six years of struggle for its retention and consolidation, our proletariat is forced to turn all its energies towards the creation of the most elementary conditions of material existence and of contact with the ABC of culture—ABC in the true and literal sense of the word. It is not for nothing that we have put to ourselves the task of having universal literacy in Russia by the tenth anniversary of the Soviet régime.

The main task of the proletarian intelligentsia in the immediate future is not the abstract formation of a new culture regardless of the absence of a basis for it, but definite culture-bearing, that is, a systematic, planful and, of course, critical imparting to the backward masses of the essential elements of the culture which already exists. It is impossible to create a class culture behind the backs of a class. And to build culture in cooperation with the working-class and in close contact with its general historic rise, one has to build Socialism, even though in the rough. In this process, the class characteristics of society will not become stronger, but, on the contrary, will begin to dissolve and to disappear in direct ratio to the success of the Revolution. The liberating significance of the dictatorship of the proletariat consists in the fact that it is temporary—for a brief period only—that it is a means of clearing the road and of laying the foundations of a society without classes and of a culture based upon solidarity.

Marx and Engels came out of the ranks of the petty bourgeois democracy and, of course, were brought up on its culture and not on the culture of the proletariat. If there had been no working-class, with its strikes, struggles, sufferings and revolts, there would, of course, have been no scientific Communism, because there would have been no historical necessity for it. But its theory was formed entirely on the basis of bourgeois culture both scientific and political, though it declared a fight to the finish upon that culture. Under the pressure of capitalistic contradictions, the universalizing thought of the bourgeois democracy, of its boldest, most honest, and most far-sighted representatives, rises to the heights of a marvelous renunciation, armed with all the critical weapons of bourgeois science. Such is the origin of Marxism.

As a matter of fact, the proletariat will reconstruct ethics as well as science radically, but he will do so after he will have constructed a new society, even though in the rough. But are we not traveling in a vicious circle? How is one to build a new society with the aid of the old science and the old morals? Here we must bring in a little dialectics, that very dialectics which we now put so uneconomically into lyric poetry and into our office bookkeeping and into our cabbage soup and into our porridge. In order to begin work, the proletarian vanguard needs certain points of departure, certain scientific methods which liberate the mind from the ideologic yoke of the bourgeoisie; it is mastering these; in part has already mastered them. It has tested its fundamental method in many battles, under various conditions. But this is a long way from proletarian science. A revolutionary class cannot stop its struggle, because the Party has not yet decided whether it should or should not accept the hypothesis of electrons and ions, the psycho-analytical theory of Freud, the new mathematical discoveries of relativity, etc. True, after it has conquered power, the proletariat will find a much greater opportunity for mastering science and for revising it. This is more easily said than done. The proletariat cannot postpone Socialist reconstruction until the time when its new scientists, many of whom are still running about in short trousers, will test and clean all the instruments and all the channels of knowledge.

The proletariat rejects what is clearly unnecessary, false and reactionary, and in the various fields of its reconstruction makes use of the methods and conclusions of present-day science, taking them necessarily with the percentage of reactionary class-alloy which is contained in them. The practical result will justify itself generally and on the whole, because such a use when controlled by a Socialist goal will gradually manage and select the methods and conclusions of the theory. And by that time there will have grown up scientists who are educated under the new conditions. At any rate, the proletariat will have to carry its Socialist reconstruction to quite a high degree, that is, provide for real material security and for the satisfaction of society culturally before it will be able to carry out a general purification of science from top to bottom. I do not mean to say by this anything against the Marxist work of criticism, which many in small circles and in seminars are trying to carry through in various fields. This work is necessary and fruitful. It should be extended and deepened in every way. But one has to maintain the Marxian sense of the measure of things to count up the specific gravity of such experiments and efforts today in relation to the general scale of our historic work.

The revolutionary poets of our period are in need of being tempered—and a moral hardening is here more inseparable from an intellectual one than anywhere else. What is necessary here is a stable, flexible, activist point of view, saturated with facts and with an artistic feeling for the world. To understand and perceive truly not in a journalistic way but to feel to the very bottom the section of time in which we live, one has to know the past of mankind, its life, its work, its struggles, its hopes, its defeats, and its achievements.

Source: Trotsky, L. *Literature and Revolution*. Transcribed by N. Vaklovisky. New York: Russell & Russell, 1957.

READING 37

The NEP Balance Sheet, 1926

Lenin's New Economic Policy reintroduced a free market in agriculture and retail trade. As the below figures show, there was a return to approximate 1913 levels of production in five years. But if so successful, why did Stalin dismantle it starting in 1928? First, there was the fact that much of Communist Party had never accepted this compromise with hated Capitalism. Critics, notably Trotsky, pointed out the problem of the "Scissors Crisis" and the increasing price gap between the agricultural and industrial sectors of the economy. The biggest problem, however, was that while the NEP was successful in restoring much of the old economy, it did not produce the capital or labor to significantly expand it. Stalin would solve that problem with collectivization and the Five Year Plans.

	1913	1921	1926
Index of Factory Output	100	20	108
Grain Harvest (millions of tons)	80	37.6	76.8
Steel (millions of tons)	4.3	.2	3.1
Coal (millions of tons)	29	8.9	27.6
Railway Tonnage (millions)	132	40	83.4 (1925)
Avg. Monthly Wages	30.5	10.1	28.6

Kulaks? Communist purists feared the rise of a class of capitalistic peasants ("kulaks") who would control agriculture. Roughly defined, a kulak was someone who leased additional land and employed additional labor to work it. The following figures show that while there was a relative increase in both categories, they represented only a small proportion of the peasantry.

	1922	1923	1924	1925
% Peasants leasing excess land:	3	3.3	4.2	6.1
% Peasants employing labor:	1	1	1.7	2

THE "SCISSORS CRISIS"

1926–27: Manufactured goods prices were roughly 300% of 1913

Agricultural prices were roughly 90% of 1913

Source: Nove, Alec. *An Economic History of the U.S.S.R.* London: Penguin, 1969.

READING 38

The Expulsion of Trotsky from the Communist Party, 1927

From 1924 through 1927, Trotsky fought a losing battle with Stalin for the heart and soul of the Communist Party. His expulsion from its ranks (along with his sometimes ally and enemy Grigory Zinoviev) on Nov. 12, 1927, was a mortal blow to his lingering political hopes, and worse was to come: banishment and expulsion from the Soviet Union by 1929. That this humiliation occurred on the 10th anniversary of the October Revolution, which Trotsky had largely planned and executed, was not an accident. The following account from the left-wing British *Manchester Guardian* (today, *The Guardian*) includes interesting details on Trotsky's defiant attitude and the insults hurled by his opponents.

Complete hostility has been declared between the orthodox wing of the Russian Communist party and the leaders of the Opposition.

It was announced in Moscow yesterday that Trotsky and Zinovieff had been excluded from the party, and that eleven other Opposition leaders had been expelled from the Central Committee. Trotsky and his supporters are defiant. The indications are that the repression of their activities by the absolutist and all powerful governing authorities will be ruthless.

The expulsion represents a decisive step toward the placing of the Opposition outside party legality, and guarantees that no Opposition voice will be heard during the party Congress.

[Their] aggressive activity in holding demonstrations during the revolutionary anniversary celebration and organising meetings of "conspirators" induced the Central and Control Committees to take immediate action.

Trotsky and Zinovieff will only be able to conduct an illegal political agitation, which may end in their imprisonment. Considering the implacable character of the fight between them and the orthodox wing, it would seem they are afraid of nothing and will continue to struggle.

Report extracted from "Pravda", of the discussion at the last plenary sitting of the Central Committee.

Trotsky complained that the Opposition had been denounced as counter-revolutionary, referring always—amid protests—to the party leaders as the "fraction". [Trotky specified] "The Stalin-Bukharin fraction, which has thrown and is throwing into the inner prison of the G.P.U. splendid party men like Vassilyev, Fishelev, and many others ... ."

Petrowski: "A disgusting speech, a Menshevist speech. Frightful!"

Trotsky: "This fraction cannot stand our presence. The present regime believes in the omnipotence of force, even against its own party."

Interrupters: Menshevik!

Trotsky: "Under Lenin's leadership the general secretariat played an altogether subordinate part. (Uproar.) The situation began to change during Lenin's illness. The choice of men by the secretariat, the grouping of Stalinists in the organsation became independent of political directives. That is why Lenin, when he saw his retirement approaching, gave the party final advice 'Get rid of Stalin, who may lead the party to schism and downfall.'" (Uproar.)

Skvorzov-Stepanov (editor of the "Izvestia"): "An old calumny!"

Thalberg: "You gossip, tale-bearer!"

Kalinin (President of the Soviet Union): "Petit-bourgeois!"

Source: Manchester Guardian, 15 November 1927.

chapter

SIX

Soviet Foreign Policy, 1917–1941

READING 39

Decree on Peace, 1917

Lenin issued the Decree on Peace shortly after the Soviet seized power in October, 1917. Pay attention to the terms of the Decree. What matters most to the Bolsheviks in this Decree? What does this Decree tell us about Lenin's expectations for a coming workers' revolution in Europe? Given that no European-wide revolution happened and the Bolsheviks were forced to sign a punitive separate treaty with the Germans, why is this Decree still significant?

The workers' and peasants' government, created by the Revolution of October 24–25 and basing itself on the Soviet of Workers', Soldiers' and Peasants' Deputies, calls upon all the belligerent peoples and their government to start immediate negotiations for a just, democratic peace.

By a just or democratic peace, for which the overwhelming majority of the working class and other working people of all the belligerent countries, exhausted, tormented and racked by the war, are craving—a peace that has been most definitely and insistently demanded by the Russian workers and peasants ever since the overthrow of the tsarist monarchy—by such a peace the government means an immediate peace without annexations (i.e., without the seizure of foreign lands, without the forcible incorporation of foreign nations) and without indemnities.

The government of Russia proposes that this kind of peace be immediately concluded by all the belligerent nations, and expresses its readiness to take all the resolute measures now, without the least delay, pending the final ratification of all the terms of such a peace by authoritative assemblies of the people's representatives of all countries and all nations.

...

The government considers it the greatest of crimes against humanity to continue this war over the issue of how to divide among the strong and rich nations the weak nationalities they have conquered, and solemnly announces its determination immediately to sign terms of peace to stop this war on the terms indicated, which are equally just for all nationalities without exception.

...

The government abolishes secret diplomacy, and, for its part, announces its firm intention to conduct all negotiations quite openly in full view of the whole people. It will proceed immediately with the full publication of the secret treaties endorsed or concluded by the government of land-owners and capitalists from February to October 25, 1917. The government proclaims the unconditional and immediate annulment of everything contained in these secret treaties insofar as it is aimed, as is mostly the case, at securing advantages and privileges for the Russian landowners and capitalists and at the retention, or extension, of the annexations made by the Great Russians.

...

While addressing this proposal for peace to the governments and peoples of all the belligerent countries, the Provisional Workers' and Peasants' Government of Russia appeals in particular also to the class-conscious workers of the three most advanced nations of mankind and the largest states participating in the present way, namely, Great Britain, France, and Germany. The workers of these countries have made the greatest contributions to the cause of progress and socialism; they have furnished the great examples of the Chartist movement in England, a number of revolutions of historic importance effected by the French proletariat, and, finally, the heroic struggle against the Anti-Socialist Law in Germany, and the prolonged, persistent and disciplined work of creating mass proletarian organizations in Germany, a work which serves as a model to the workers of the whole world. All these examples of proletarian heroism and historical creative work are a pledge that the workers of the countries mentioned will understand the duty that now faces them of saving mankind from the horrors of war and its consequences, that these workers, by comprehensive, determined, and supremely vigorous action, will help us to conclude peace successfully, and at the same time emancipate the laboring and exploited masses of our population from all forms of slavery and all forms of exploitation.

Source: Lenin, V.I. *Collected Works*, 4th English Edition, Vol. 35. Translated by Jim Riordan. Moscow: Progress Publishers, 1972.

READING 40

Lenin's Address Urging Acceptance of the Brest-Litovsk Peace Treaty, 1918

In the early months of 1918, the new Soviet government stalled in signing a peace treaty with the Germans. It hoped that an improved position on the battlefield would give the government more power at the negotiating table. The plan backfired and Soviet losses continued. Finally, in February, Lenin decided that it had to settle for peace regardless of how terrible the terms were. In this excerpt, he justifies this decision. What are Lenin's justifications for signing the treaty? What do the phrases "revolutionary cant" and "the objective correlation of class forces and material factors" mean? What message is Lenin trying to send to his listeners?

The German reply offers peace terms still more severe than those of Brest-Litovsk. Nevertheless, I am absolutely convinced that to refuse to sign these terms is only possible for those who are intoxicated by revolutionary phrases. Up till now I have tried to impress on the members of the party the necessity of clearing their minds of revolutionary cant. Now I must do this openly, for unfortunately my worst forebodings have been justified.

Party workers in January declared war on revolutionary phrases, and said that a policy of refusal to sign a peace would perhaps satisfy the craving for effectiveness, but would leave out of account the objective correlation of class forces and material factors in the present initial moment of the Socialist revolution. They further said that if we refused to sign the peace then proposed more crushing defeats would compel Russia to conclude a still more disadvantageous separate peace.

The event proved even worse than I anticipated, for our retreating army seems demoralized and absolutely refuses to fight. Only unrestrained phrasemaking can impel Russia at this moment and in these conditions to continue the war, and I personally would not remain a minute longer either in the Government or in the Central Committee of our party if the policy of phrasemaking were to prevail.

This new bitter truth has revealed itself with such terrible distinctness that it is impossible not to see it. All the bourgeoisie in Russia is jubilant at the approach of the Germans. Only a blind man or men infatuated by phrases can fail to see that the policy of a revolutionary war without an army is water in the bourgeois mill. In the bourgeois papers there is already exaltation in view of the impending overthrow of the Soviet Government by the Germans.

We are compelled to submit to a distressing peace. It will not stop revolution in Germany and Europe. We shall now begin to prepare a revolutionary army, not by phrases and exclamations, as did those who after January 10th did nothing even to attempt to stop our fleeing troops, but by organized work, by the creation of a serious national, mighty army.

Their knees are on our chest, and our position is hopeless. This peace must be accepted as a respite enabling us to prepare a decisive resistance to the bourgeoisie and imperialists. The proletariat of the whole world will come to our aid. Then we shall renew the fight.

Source: Lenin, V.I. "Lenin for Surrender," *Current History,* Vol 8, No. 1. New York: The New York Times Company, 1918.

READING 41

Left Communists Condemn the Brest-Litovsk Treaty, 1918

Not everyone was happy with Lenin's decision. In this excerpt, Soviet Communists respond. What argument do they make? What are they and Lenin really fighting about in this debate?

In response to the offensive by the German imperialists, openly declaring their aim of crushing the proletarian revolution in Russia, the party's CC responded by agreeing to make peace on those conditions that a few days earlier had been rejected by the Soviet delegation at Brest. This agreement, accepted on the first onslaught of the enemies of the proletariat, represents the capitulation by the leading section of the international proletariat before the international bourgeoisie ... .

We consider that after seizing power, after the complete crushing of the last bastions of the bourgeoisie, there inevitably arises before the proletariat the task of fomenting civil war on an international scale, a task for whose fulfilment it cannot stop in the face of any danger. Refusal to fulfil this will lead to its destruction by internal degeneration, the equivalent of suicide ... .

Source: Protokoly TsK RSDRP(b): avgust 1917-fevral' 1918. Moscow: Politizdat, 1958.

READING 42

Thesis on the Condition of Admission to the Communist International, 1918

The Comintern, or the Third International, was created in 1919. It was a Soviet-sponsored international organization whose purpose was to fight for world Communism. It lasted until 1943 when Stalin disbanded it in order to avoid antipathy from the United States during the nascent Cold War. In this excerpt, the Comintern lays out the conditions for membership and its larger mission. As you read this, think about how the Comintern understood the role of the press in the Communist world. What are the obligations of Comintern members? What is the Comintern's position on Colonialism? What is the importance of the rule of law for the Comintern? Where can you see Lenin's ideas about the "Vanguard" in this document? What is the Comintern's understanding of the peasantry and its role in the revolution? What potential problems can you see in this document for the protection of individual civil rights?

1. All propaganda and agitation must bear a really communist character and correspond to the programme and decisions of the Communist International. All the party's press organs must be run by reliable communists who have proved their devotion to the cause of the proletariat. The dictatorship of the proletariat must not be treated simply as a current formula learnt off by heart. Propaganda for it must be carried out in such a way that its necessity is comprehensible to every simple worker, every woman worker, every soldier and peasant from the facts of their daily lives, which must be observed systematically by our press and used day by day.

    The periodical and other press and all the party's publishing institutions must be subordinated to the party leadership, regardless of whether, at any given moment, the party as a whole is legal or illegal. The publishing houses must not be allowed to abuse their independence and pursue policies that do not entirely correspond to the policies of the party.

    In the columns of the press, at public meetings, in the trades unions, in the co-operatives—wherever the members of the Communist International can gain admittance—it is necessary to brand not only the bourgeoisie but also its helpers, the reformists of every shade, systematically and pitilessly.

2. Every organization that wishes to affiliate to the Communist International must regularly and methodically remove reformists and centrists from every responsible post in the labor movement (party organizations, editorial boards, trades unions, parliamentary factions, co-operatives, local government) and replace them with tested communists, without worrying unduly about the fact that, particularly at first, ordinary workers from the masses will be replacing 'experienced' opportunists.

3. In almost every country in Europe and America the class struggle is entering the phase of civil war. Under such conditions the communists can place no trust in bourgeois legality. They have the obligation of setting up a parallel organizational apparatus which, at the decisive moment, can assist the party to do its duty to the revolution. In every country where a state of siege or emergency laws deprive the communists of the opportunity of carrying on all their work legally, it is absolutely necessary to combine legal and illegal activity.

...

4. A particularly marked and clear attitude on the question of the colonies and oppressed nations is necessary on the part of the communist parties of those countries whose bourgeoisies are in possession of colonies and oppress other nations. Every party that wishes to belong to the Communist International has the obligation of exposing the dodges of its 'own' imperialists in the colonies, of supporting every liberation movement in the colonies not only in words but in deeds, of demanding that their imperialist compatriots should be thrown out of the colonies, of cultivating in the hearts of the workers in their own country a truly fraternal relationship to the working population in the colonies and to the oppressed nations, and of carrying out systematic propaganda among their own country's troops against any oppression of colonial peoples.

...

5. Parties that wish to belong to the Communist International have the obligation to subject the personal composition of their parliamentary factions to review, to remove all unreliable elements from them and to subordinate these factions to the party leadership, not only in words but also in deeds, by calling on every individual communist member of parliament to subordinate the whole of his activity to the interests of really revolutionary propaganda and agitation.

6. The parties belonging to the Communist International must be built on the basis of the principle of *democratic centralism*. In the present epoch of acute civil war the communist party will only be able to fulfil its duty if it is organized in as centralist a manner as possible, if iron discipline reigns within it and if the party center, sustained by the confidence of the party membership, is endowed with the fullest rights and authority and the most far-reaching powers.

7. The communist parties of those countries in which the communists can carry out their work legally must from time to time undertake purges (re-registration) of the membership of their party organizations in order to cleanse the party systematically of the petty-bourgeois elements within it.

8. Every party that wishes to belong to the Communist International has the obligation to give unconditional support to every soviet republic in its struggle against the forces of counter-revolution. The communist parties

must carry out clear propaganda to prevent the transport of war material to the enemies of the soviet republics. They must also carry out legal or illegal propaganda, etc., with every means at their disposal among troops sent to stifle workers' republics.

...

9. All the leading press organs of the parties in every country have the duty of printing all the important official documents of the Executive Committee of the Communist International.

Source: Lenin, V.I. *Collected Works*, 4th English Edition, Vol. 31. Translated by Jim Riordan. Moscow: Progress Publishers, 1965.

READING 43

Trotsky and Permanent Revolution, 1906

This short excerpt deals with the question of world revolution which the Bolsheviks believed was critical to the success of a Communist revolution in Russia. Trotsky wrote this paragraph in 1906 just after the 1905 Revolution. How does Trotsky talk about the peasantry in this piece? Why does world revolution matter so much to him and the other Bolsheviks?

Left to its own resources, the working class of Russia will inevitably be crushed by the counter-revolution the moment the peasantry turns its back on it. It will have no alternative but to link the fate of its political rule, and, hence, the fate of the whole Russian revolution, with the fate of the socialist revolution in Europe. That colossal state-political power ... will cast itself into the scales of the class struggle of the entire capitalist world. With state power in its hands, with counter-revolution behind it and European reaction in front of it, it will send forth to its comrades the world over the old rallying cry, which this time will be a call for the last attack: *Workers of all countries, unite!*

Source: Trotsky, L. *Permanent Revolution and Results and Prospects.* Edited by Kunal Chattopadhyay et all. Translated by J. Fineberg. Delhi: Akaar Books, 2005.

READING 44

Lenin, "On the Slogan for a United States of Europe," 1915

Lenin revisited the question of world revolution in 1915. What vision of the future is Lenin painting here? What does Lenin think will happen to nations as the revolution spreads? What might the long-term consequences of this be, not just for the Soviet Union, but also for setting the stage for the Cold War?

Uneven economic and political development is an absolute law of capitalism. Hence, the victory of socialism is possible first in several or even in one capitalist country alone. After expropriating the capitalists and organizing their own socialist production, the victorious proletariat of that country will arise against the rest of the world—the capitalist world—attracting to its cause the oppressed classes of other countries, stirring uprisings in those countries against the capitalists. The political form of a society wherein the proletariat is victorious in overthrowing the bourgeoisie will be a democratic republic, which will more and more concentrate the forces of the proletariat of a given nation or nations in the struggle against states that have not yet gone over to socialism. The abolition of classes is impossible without a dictatorship of the oppressed class, of the proletariat. A free union of nations in socialism is impossible without a more or less prolonged and stubborn struggle of the socialist republics against the backward states.

Source: Lenin, V.I. *Collected Works*, 4th English Edition, Vol. 21. Translated by Jim Riordan. Progress Publishers, Moscow, 1963.

READING 45

Lenin, "Letter to American Workers," 1918

Lenin wrote this famous letter to the workers of America during the Russian Civil War. In this excerpt, you can see many of the core beliefs that defined the Bolsheviks and their understanding of the Revolution. As you read this, put yourself in the shoes of an American worker living in Chicago in 1918. Imagine that your pay is low, that you struggle to feed and house your family, and that your working conditions are dangerous. Does this letter resonate with you? If so, why and how? What does Lenin have to say here about the ends justifying the means and the way that history will someday view the Russian Revolution? How does Lenin talk about the American Revolution and the Civil War, and why does he use this tactic? Lastly, what does freedom look like for Lenin, and how does it differ from a traditional liberal understanding of the term?

The history of modern, civilized America opened with one of those great, really liberating, really revolutionary wars of which there have been so few compared to the vast number of wars of conquest which, like the present imperialist war, were caused by squabbles among kings, landowners or capitalists over the division of usurped lands or ill-gotten gains. That was the war the American people waged against the British robbers who oppressed America and held her in colonial slavery, in the same way as these "civilized" bloodsuckers are still oppressing and holding in colonial slavery hundreds of millions of people in India, Egypt, and all parts of the world.

About 150 years have passed since then. Bourgeois civilization has borne all its luxurious fruits. America has taken first place among the free and educated nations in level of development of the productive forces of collective human endeavor, in the utilization of machinery and of all the wonders of modern engineering. At the same time, America has become one of the foremost countries in regard to the depth of the abyss which lies between the handful of arrogant multimillionaires who wallow in filth and luxury, and the millions of working people who constantly live on the verge of pauperism.

…

The American multimillionaires … have profited more than all the rest. They have converted all, even the richest, countries into their tributaries.

They have grabbed hundreds of billions of dollars. And every dollar is sullied with filth … . Every dollar is sullied with the filth of "profitable" war contracts, which in every country made the rich richer and the poor poorer. And every dollar is stained with blood—from that ocean of blood that has been shed by the ten million killed and twenty million maimed in the great, noble, liberating and holy war to decide whether the British or the German robbers are to get most of the spoils, whether the British or the German thugs are to be *foremost* in throttling the weak nations all over the world … .

…

The representatives of the bourgeoisie understand that for the sake of overthrowing Negro slavery, of overthrowing the rule of the slave-owners, it was worth letting the country go through long years of civil war, through the abysmal ruin, destruction and terror that accompany every war. But now, when we are confronted with the vastly greater task of overthrowing capitalist *wage*-slavery, of overthrowing the rule of the bourgeoisie—now, the representatives and defenders of the bourgeoisie, and also the reformist socialists who have been frightened by the bourgeoisie and are shunning the revolution, cannot and do not want to understand that civil war is necessary and legitimate.

…

The British bourgeoisie have forgotten their 1649, the French bourgeoisie have forgotten their 1793. Terror was just and legitimate when the bourgeoisie resorted to it for their own benefit against feudalism. Terror became monstrous and criminal when the workers and poor peasants dared to use it against the bourgeoisie! Terror was just and legitimate when used for the purpose of substituting one exploiting minority for another exploiting minority. Terror became monstrous and criminal when it began to be used for the purpose of overthrowing *every* exploiting minority, to be used in the interests of the vast actual majority, in the interests of the proletariat and semi-proletariat, the working class and the poor peasants! The international imperialist bourgeoisie have slaughtered ten million men and maimed twenty million in "their" war, the war to decide whether the British or the German vultures are to rule the world.

If *our* war, the war of the oppressed and exploited against the oppressors and the exploiters, results in half a million or a million casualties in all countries, the bourgeoisie will say that the former casualties are justified, while the latter are criminal.

The proletariat will have something entirely different to say.

The truth is that no revolution can be successful unless *the resistance of the exploiters is crushed*. When we, the workers and toiling peasants, captured state power, it became our duty to crush the resistance of the exploiters.

…

That is why we are all so firmly convinced that no matter what misfortunes may still be in store for it, our Republic of Soviets is *invincible*.

It is invincible because every blow struck by frenzied imperialism, every defeat the international bourgeoisie inflict on us, rouses more and more sections of the workers and peasants to the struggle, teaches them at the cost of enormous sacrifice, steels them and engenders new heroism on a mass scale.

Source: Lenin, V.I. *Collected Works*, 4th English Edition, Vol. 28. Translated by Jim Riordan. Moscow: Progress Publishers, 1965.

READING 46

Stalin, "The October Revolution and the Tactics of the Russian Communists," 1924

In this excerpt, we see the foundations of Stalin's argument for "Socialism in one country" and against Trotsky's belief in permanent revolution. How does Stalin lean on the legacy of the now-dead Lenin to make this argument? Why is it so critical for Stalin that he set forth this argument? How might the leaders of Western governments have understood this piece?

According to Lenin, the revolution draws its strength primarily from among the workers and peasants of Russia itself. According to Trotsky, the necessary strength can be found only "in the arena of the world proletarian revolution."

But what if the world revolution is fated to arrive with some delay? Is there any ray of hope for our revolution? Trotsky sees no ray of hope, for "the contradictions in the position of a workers' government ... can be solved *only* ... in the arena of the world proletarian revolution." According to this plan, there is but one prospect left for our revolution: to vegetate in its own contradictions and rot away while waiting for the world revolution ... .

"Permanent revolution" is not a mere underestimation of the revolutionary potentialities of the peasant movement. "Permanent revolution" is an underestimation of the peasant movement which leads to the repudiation of Lenin's theory of the dictatorship of the proletariat ... .

In his study of imperialism, especially in the period of the war, Lenin arrived at the law of the uneven, spasmodic economic and political development of the capitalist countries. According to this law, the development of enterprises, trusts, branches of industry and individual countries proceeds not evenly—not according to an established order of rotation, not in such a way that one trust, one branch of industry or one country is always in advance of the others, while other trusts or countries keep regularly one behind the other—but spasmodically, with interruptions in the development of some countries and leaps ahead in the development of others. Under these circumstances the "quite legitimate" striving of the countries that have slowed down to hold their old positions and the equally "legitimate" striving of the countries that have leapt ahead to seize new positions lead to a situation in which armed clashes among the imperialist countries are inevitable. Such was the case, for example, with Germany, which half a century ago was a backward country in comparison with France and England. The same must be said of Japan as compared with Russia. It is well known, however, that by the beginning of the twentieth century Germany and Japan had leapt so far ahead that Germany had succeeded in overtaking France and had begun to press England hard on the world market, while Japan was pressing Russia. As is well known, it was from these contradictions that the recent imperialist war arose … .

The opportunists of all countries assert that the proletarian revolution can begin—if it is to begin anywhere at all, according to their theory—only in industrially developed countries, and that the more highly developed these countries are industrially the more chances are there for the victory of socialism. Moreover, according to them, the possibility of the victory of socialism in one country, and in a country little developed in the capitalist sense at that, is excluded as something absolutely improbable. As far back as the period of the war, Lenin, taking as his basis the law of the uneven development of the imperialist states, proposed to the opportunists his theory of the proletarian revolution of the victory of socialism in one country, even if that country is less developed in the capitalist sense.

It is well known that the October Revolution has fully confirmed the correctness of Lenin's theory of the proletarian revolution.

…

It goes without saying that for the *complete* victory of socialism, for *complete* security against the restoration of the old order, the united efforts of the proletarians of several countries are necessary.

It goes without saying that we need support. But what does support of our revolution by the West-European proletariat imply? Is not the sympathy of European workers for our revolution, their readiness to thwart the imperialists' plans of intervention—is not all this support? Is this not real assistance? Of course it is. If it had not been for this support, if it had not been for this assistance, not only from the European workers but also from the colonial and dependent countries, the proletarian dictatorship in Russia would have been in a tight corner.

Has this sympathy and this assistance, coupled with the might of our Red Army and the readiness of the workers and peasants of Russia to defend their socialist fatherland to the last—has all this been sufficient to beat off the attacks of the imperialists and to win us the necessary conditions for the serious work of construction? Yes, it has been sufficient.

Is this sympathy growing stronger, or is it ebbing away? Undoubtedly, it is growing stronger.

Hence, have we favorable conditions, not only to push on with the organization of socialist economy, but also, in our turn, to give support to the West-European workers and to the oppressed peoples of the East? Yes, we have. This is eloquently proved by the seven years' history of the proletarian dictatorship in Russia.

Can it be denied that a mighty wave of labor enthusiasm has already risen in our country? No, it cannot be denied.

After all this, what does Trotsky's assertion that a revolutionary Russia could not hold its own against a conservative Europe signify? It can signify only this: first, that Trotsky does not appreciate the inherent strength of our revolution; secondly, that Trotsky does not understand the inestimable importance of the moral support which is given to our revolution by the workers of the west and the peasants of the east; thirdly, that Trotsky does not perceive the internal cancer which is eating at the heart of imperialism today … .

Source: Stalin, I.V. *Problems of Leninism*. Translated by Charles Farrell. Moscow: Foreign Languages Publishing House, 1977.

READING 47

"The Struggle Against Imperialist War and the Tasks of the Communists," 1932

After you read this excerpt from the Comintern in 1932, ask yourself how the Comintern understood the international situation in 1932 and the Soviet Union's role in it. How accurate were they?

Ten years after the world war, the big imperialist powers solemnly conclude a pact for outlawing war: they talk about disarmament; they seek, with the support of the leaders of international Social Democracy, to delude the workers and toiling masses into the belief that the rule of monopoly capitalism assures peace to the world … .

The changes in the world situation since then are characterized by a tremendous intensification of all the contradictions of capitalism, by the great economic and political strengthening of the Soviet Union, by the rapid growth of the national revolutionary movements in the colonies and semi-colonial countries—above all in China, and by the intensification of the class struggle between the bourgeoisie and the proletariat in the capitalist countries.

The antagonisms between the imperialist powers in the struggle for markets are more and more sharply expressed. But still stronger … is the principle antagonism that is dividing the world into two camps: on the one hand the whole of the capitalist world, and on the other hand the U.S.S.R., around which the international proletariat and the oppressed peoples of the colonies are grouping.

The fight for the destruction of the Soviet system and the Chinese revolution, for unrestricted domination over China and for possession of the enormous reservoirs of raw materials and the markets in these countries, is … the basis for the imminent danger of a new imperialist war that is threatening at the present time. The coming imperialist world war will not only be a mechanized war with a tremendous use of material, but simultaneously it will be a war that will seize upon vast millions, indeed upon the majority of the population of the warring countries. The boundary between battlefront and home front will … become obliterated.

Source: Resolution of the VI World Congress of the Communist International, July-August, 1928. New York: Workers Library Publishers, 1932.

READING 48

Vyacheslav Molotov Radio Announcement of the Soviet Occupation of Eastern Poland, 1939

In this short radio announcement, airing on September 1, 1939, Molotov announced the movement of Soviet troops into Poland, thus fulfilling the terms of the secret agreement that the Soviets had made with the Nazis. What was happening in western Poland on this day in 1939? What kind of language does Molotov use to justify this action? In these months, the Soviet army arrested 20,000 Polish officers and then executed them in the Katyn Forest near Smolensk.

The USSR government this morning handed a note to the Polish ambassador in Moscow which announced that the Soviet government directed the Supreme Command of the Red Army to order their forces to cross the border and to undertake the defense of the life and property of the population of western Ukraine and western Belorussia.

The Soviet government also declared in the note that it is simultaneously resolved to undertake all measures to free the Polish people from the ill-fated war into which it was dragged by its unwise leadership, and to give it the possibility to begin to live a peaceful life.

Source: Sakwa, Richard (ed). "The Soviet Occupation of Eastern Poland," *The Rise and Fall of the Soviet Union, 1917–1991*. New York: Taylor and Francis, 2005. Copyright © 2005 by Taylor & Francis Group.

READING 49

Winston Churchill's Broadcast to the British People, 1939

Churchill gave this speech, which was his first wartime broadcast, shortly after the USSR occupied Poland. In it, he tries to talk to the British people about what the Soviets are doing and why. How does he explain it? Does he leave any space for hope that the Soviets might eventually side with the Allies?

Poland has been again overrun by two of the great Powers which held it in bondage for the last 150 years, but were unable to conquer the spirit of the Polish nation. The heroic defense of Warsaw shows that the soul of Poland is indestructible and that she will rise again like a rock, which may for a spell be submerged by a tidal wave, but which remains a rock .... Russia has pursued a cold policy of self-interest. We could have wished that the Russian armies should be standing on their present lines as the friends of the allies in Poland, instead of as invaders. But that the Russian armies should stand on this line was clearly necessary for the safety of Russia against the Nazi menace .... I cannot forecast to you the action of Russia. It is a riddle wrapped in mystery inside an enigma; but perhaps there is a key. That key is Russian national interest .... It cannot be in accordance with the interest or safety of Russia that Nazi Germany should plant itself upon the shores of the Black Sea, or that is should overrun the Balkan States and subjugate the Slavonic peoples of south-eastern Europe. That would be contrary to the historic life-interests of Russia. But in this quarter of the world, the South East of Europe, these interests of Russia fall into the same channel as the interests of Britain and France.

Source: Churchill, Winston. *The Soul of Poland is Indestructible*. London: Curtis Brown Ltd., 1939.

READING 50

A Propaganda Leaflet Dropped from Soviet Airplanes During the First Days of the Winter War, 1939

In an effort to protect the Soviet Union's western flank, Stalin gave the order to invade Finland on November 30, 1939. Soviet pilots, soldiers, and political commissars distributed these pamphlets to the Finnish people. What is the message in this pamphlet? What age-old propaganda tools are they using here? Do you think it worked?

The toiling people of Finland!
Workers, working women, peasants!
Soldiers of the Finnish army!
You will be evicted from your homes and thrown under the open sky. Your homes will be burned, your properties will be destroyed, and your whole lives will be plunged into misery. Your mothers, wives, sisters, children will be turned to homeless beggars. With one blow the fruits of people's lifelong work will be destroyed. The century-long culture of the Finnish people will be wrecked … . The bunch of generals, financiers, manor owners and capitalists trample down the freedom and culture of Finland in people's blood and anguish simultaneously when the imperialistic foreign masters of this gang of traitors rub their hands with pleasure … .

It is time to finish the banditry of the renegade oppressors of the people. Do not let your homes be burned! Workers! Do not let your factories be burned! Soldiers! Turn your weapons against the destroyers of your home stoves! Go over to the [Soviet sponsored] People's Government. This government brings peace to the country! It has concluded a treaty of mutual assistance and friendship between the Soviet Union and the Democratic Republic of Finland. This treaty secures the independence of Finland, it secures a peaceful life and flourishment of the Finnish people. It relieves you from the horrors and destruction of the war.

Long live the people of free Finland and its Democratic Government!

Source: Soviet Department for Agitation and Propaganda, "Propaganda Leaflet Dropped From Soviet Airplanes During the First Days of the Winter War," Translated by Pauli Kruhse, 1939.

READING 51

The Katyn Massacre, 1940

In this, one of the most disgraceful incidents of the Second World War, Stalin decides to deal with the 20,000 arrested Polish officers who were captured in the first days of the Polish invasion in 1939. What justifications does Beria give for their execution? Can you do some extra research to find out what happened when the Nazis discovered the Polish officers' bodies in mass graves in the Katyn Forest in April, 1943?

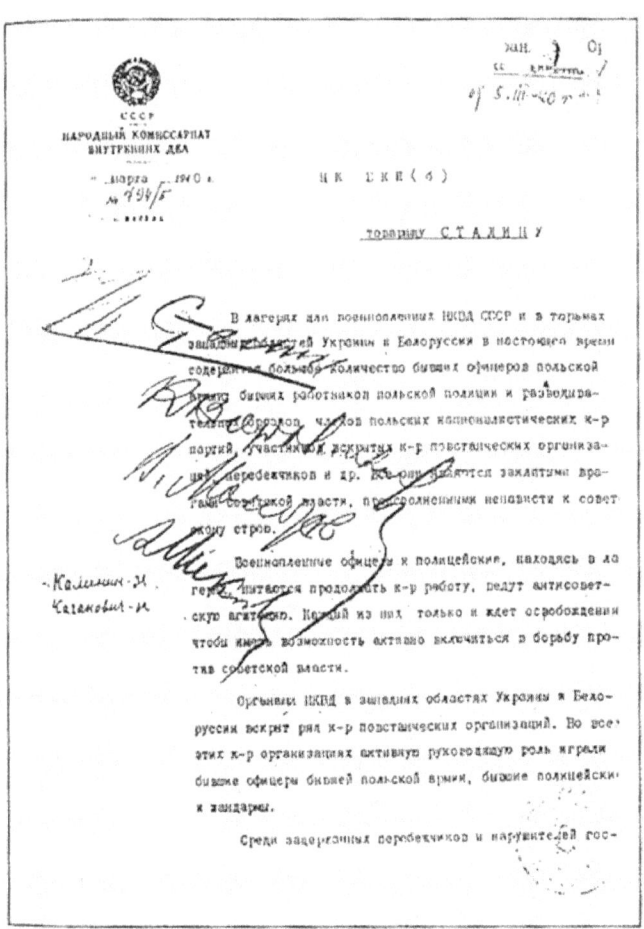

"USSR
PEOPLE'S COMMISSARIAT OF INTERNAL AFFAIRS
March 1940
No. 794/B
Moscow

TOP SECRET
Central Committee, VKP(b)
TO COMRADE STALIN

A large quantity of former officials of the Polish Army, employees of the Polish Police and intelligence services, members of the Polish Nationalistic Party, counter-revolutionaries, discovered members pertaining to insurgent groups of counter-revolutionaries, fugitive and others, all of them sworn enemies of the Soviet régime, who hate the Soviet system, are at the moment in prisoners of war field camps of the NKVD OF THE USSR and in prisons of Ukraine and Byelorussia.

The prisoners of war and policemen in field camps conduct anti-Soviet agitation. Each one of them is only hoping and awaits release in order to have the capability actively to be included in activities against the Soviet régime.

The organs of the NKVD in the western provinces of Ukraine and Byelorussia have discovered a number of insurgent counter-revolutionary organizations.

Former officials of the former Polish Army and policemen, as well as of gendarmerie have shown that they are participating in espionage and insurgent activities. Among the prisoners (without considering the soldiers and officials composition) there are 14,736 former officials, government civil employees, landowners, police, gendarmes, prison guards, colonizers of border regions and intelligence officials – by nationality more than 97% are Polish … .

On the basis of the fact that they all are declared enemies of the Soviet régime, the NKVD OF THE USSR considers it necessary:

I. To authorize the NKVD OF THE USSR: in the matters about the prisoners of war in field camps of 14,700 people of former Polish officials, landowners, policemen, civil employees of government, intelligence officials, gendarmes, colonizers of the border regions and prison guards and also the matter about those arrested and located in prisons in the western regions of Ukraine and Byelorussia in a quantity of 11,000 people, insurgents, spies and saboteurs, former landowners, factory owners, former Polish police officials, fugitive civil employees of government, the highest method of punishment due to apply to them—execution.

PEOPLES COMMISSIONER OF
THE INTERNAL AFFAIRS
Of the Union OF SSR
(signature) L. Beria"

Source: People's Commissariat of Internal Affairs. NKVD Letter No 00974/B. Wikisource, 1940.

chapter

SEVEN
Stalinism as a Way of Life

READING 52

Stalin on the Grain Crisis, 1928

In 1928, Stalin announced the adoption of the First Five Year Plan. It centered on the rapid industrialization of the country and the collectivization of agriculture. This would come to be called the "Revolution from Above" and marked a distinct turn away from the limited privatization of the New Economic Policy. One of the reasons that the First Five Year Plan was announced was that the Soviet Union experienced a crisis in grain procurements in 1928. In the speech that follows, Stalin explains what he understands to be the cause of the current grain crisis and what he believes needs to be done to fix it. How does Stalin understand the causes of the crisis? What is Stalin's perspective on the importance of heavy industry? Does any of Stalin's argument seem reasonable to you? Before reading on, can you predict what this kind of declaration would mean for the peasantry of the Soviet Union?

… The underlying cause of our grain difficulties is that the increase in the production of grain for the market is not keeping pace with the increase in the demand for grain.

Industry is growing. The number of workers is growing. Towns are growing. And, lastly, the regions producing industrial crops (cotton, flax, sugar beet, etc.) are growing, creating a demand for grain. All this leads to a rapid increase in our requirements as regards grain—grain available for the market. But the production of grain for the market is increasing at a disastrously slow rate … .

How … is it to be explained that … the amount of grain we are producing for the market is only one-half, and the amount we are exporting is only about one-twentieth of what it was in previous times?

The reason is primarily and chiefly the change in the structure of our agriculture brought about by the October Revolution, the change from landlord and large-scale kulak farming, which provided the portion of marketed grain, to small- and middle-peasant farming, which provides the smallest proportion of marketed grain … .

The abolition of landlord (large-scale) farming [and] the reduction of the kulak (large-scale) farming to less than one-third … was bound to lead, and in fact has led, to a sharp reduction in the output of grain for the market as compared with prewar times. It is a fact that the amount of marketed grain in our country is now half of what it was before the war, although the gross output of grain has reached the prewar level ... .

What is the way out of this situation?

Some people see the way out of this situation in a return to kulak farming, in the development and extension of kulak farming. These people dare not advocate a return to landlord farming, for they realize, evidently, that such talk is dangerous in our times. All the more eagerly, therefore, do they urge the necessity of the utmost development of kulak farming in the interest of Soviet power. These people think that Soviet power can simultaneously rely on two opposite classes—the class of the kulaks, whose economic principle is the exploitation of the working class, and the class of the workers, whose economic principle is the abolition of all exploitation.

A trick worthy of reactionaries.

There is no need to prove that these reactionary "plans" have nothing in common with the interests of the working class, with the principles of Marxism, with the tasks of Leninism ... .

What, then, is the way out of the situation?

1. The way out lies, firstly in the transition from the small, backward and scattered peasant farms to amalgamated, large-scale socialized farms, equipped with machinery, armed with scientific knowledge and capable of producing a maximum of grain for the market. The solution lies in the transition from individual peasant farming to collective, socialized farming.

    ...

2. Finally, the way out lies in systematically increasing the yield of the small and middle individual peasant farms. We cannot and should not lend any support to the individual large kulak farms. But we can and should assist the individual small- and middle-peasant farms, helping them to increase their crop yields and drawing them into the channel of cooperative organizations ... .

Thus, if all these tasks are fulfilled, the state can in three or four years' time have at its disposal 250,000,000 to 300,000,000 additional poods of marketable grain—a supply more or less sufficient to enable us to maneuver within the country as well as abroad ... .

Should not, in addition to these measures, a number of other measures be adopted—measures, say, to reduce the rate of development of our industry, the growth of which is causing a considerable increase in the demand for grain which at present is outstripping the increase in the production of grain for the market? No, not under any circumstances! To reduce the rate of development of industry would mean to weaken the working class; for every step forward in the development of industry, every new factory, every new works, is, as Lenin expressed it, "a new stronghold" of the working class, which strengthens its position in the fight against the petty-bourgeois element, in the fight against the capitalist elements in our economy ... .

Should we, perhaps, for the sake of greater "caution," retard the development of heavy industry and make light industry, which produces chiefly for the peasant market, the basis of our industry as a whole? Not under any circumstances! That would be suicidal; it would undermine our whole industry, including light industry. It would mean abandoning the slogan of industrializing our country, it would transform our country into an appendage of the world capitalist system of economy ... .

Source: Stalin, I.V. *Problems of Leninism*. Moscow: Foreign Language Publishers, 1934, 248–249.

READING 53

Stalin's "On the Liquidation of the Kulaks as a Class," 1929

Stalin's first response to the grain crisis in 1928 was to return to forced grain requisitioning in the countryside and to increase production targets for state industry as a part of the First Five Year Plan. Those who opposed this plan, notably Bukharin, became known as the "Right Opposition." Then, in 1929, Stalin called for the full collectivization of the countryside. To prepare the ground for this plan, he called for the "liquidation of the kulaks as a class." This is the speech where Stalin announced his plan. In subsequent years, nearly two million "kulaks" (who were often no better off than everyone else) were deported and sent to "special settlements" to work. Forced collectivization became a reality across the grain-producing parts of the Soviet Union. In this excerpt, what justifications does Stalin give for his decision to go after the "kulaks"? How does Stalin characterize the people he labels as "kulaks," and who bears responsibility for this liquidation?

... Can we advance our socialized industry at an accelerated rate as long as we have an agricultural base such as is provided by small-peasant farming, which is incapable of expanded reproduction, and which, in addition, is the predominant force in our national economy? No, we cannot.

Can Soviet power and the work of socialist construction rest for any length of time on two different foundations: on the most large-scale and concentrated socialist industry, and the most scattered and backward, small-commodity peasant farming? No, they cannot. Sooner or later this would be bound to end in the complete collapse of the whole national economy.

What, then, is the solution? The solution lies in enlarging the agricultural units, in making agriculture capable of accumulation, of expanded reproduction, and in thus transforming the agricultural bases of our national economy ... .

The characteristic feature in the work of our Party during the past year is that we, as a Party, as the Soviet power,

a. have developed an offensive along the whole front against the capitalist elements in the countryside;
b. that this offensive, as you know, has brought about and is bringing about very palpable, positive results.

What does this mean? It means that we have passed from the policy of restricting the exploiting proclivities of the kulaks to the policy of eliminating the kulaks as a class. This means that we have made, and are still making, one of the decisive turns in our whole policy … .

Now we are able to carry on a determined offensive against the kulaks, to break their resistance, to eliminate them as a class and substitute for their output the output of the collective farms and state farms. Now, the kulaks are being expropriated by the masses of poor and middle peasants themselves, by the masses who are putting solid collectivization into practice. Now, the expropriation of the kulaks in the regions of solid collectivization is no longer just an administrative measure. Now, the expropriation of the kulaks is an integral part of the formation and development of the collective farms. Consequently it is now ridiculous and foolish to discourse on the expropriation of the kulaks. You do not lament the loss of the hair of one who has been beheaded.

There is another question which seems no less ridiculous: whether the kulaks should be permitted to join the collective farms. Of course not, for they are sworn enemies of the collective-farm movement … .

Source: Stalin, I.V. *Problems of Leninism*. Moscow: Foreign Language Publishers, 1934.

READING 54

On the Rate of Collectivization and State Assistance for Collective-Farm Construction, 1930

Read this excerpt with a critical eye. Refer back to your other texts to uncover whether or not the forced grain requisitioning and collectivization went well. Was collectivization easy or was it violent and difficult? What are the claims made here? Are they accurate? If there are inaccuracies, why did the Central Committee make them? What conclusions does the Central Committee draw from its observations? What is missing from this report in terms of thinking about the peasants, their acts of resistance, and the human cost?

1. In recent months the collectivization movement has taken another step forward and has embraced not only separate groups of individual households, but also entire raions, okrugs and even oblasts and krais. The movement is based on collectivization of the means of production of poor and middle-peasant households.

   All the rates of development of the collectivization movement envisaged by the plan have been surpassed. By the spring of 1930 the sown area worked on a communal basis will be significantly more than 30 million hectares, i.e., the five-year collectivization plan, which envisaged a coverage of 22–24 million hectares for the collectives towards the end of the five-year period, will already be significantly over-fulfilled this year.

   We therefore have the material base for replacing large-scale kulak production by large-scale collective-farm production, and for making a mighty stride forward towards the creation of a socialist agriculture, not to mention state farming, the growth of which is significantly overtaking all the planned objectives.

   This circumstance, which has a decisive significance for the whole economy of the USSR, has given the Party every right to switch, in its practical work, from a policy of limiting the exploiting tendencies of the kulaks to one of liquidating the kulaks as a class.

2. It may be established without any doubt on the basis of all this that within the limits of the five-year plan, instead of collectivization

of 20 percent of the sown area as envisaged by that plan, we can solve the problem of collectivizing the overwhelming majority of peasant households. At the same time the collectivization of such important grain areas as the Lower Volga, the Middle Volga, and the North Caucasus may be basically completed by the autumn of 1930, or in any case by the spring of 1931; the collectivization of other grain areas may be basically finished by the autumn of 1931, or in any case by the spring of 1932 ... .

Source: Malin, V.N. and A. V. Korobov (eds.), *Direktivy KPSS i sovetskogo pravitel'stva po khoziaistvennym voprosam*. Vol 2. Moscow, 1957, 137. Taken from Matthews, Mervyn ed., *Soviet Government: a selection of official documents on internal policies*. New York: Taplinger, 1974.

READING 55

Stalin's "Dizzy With Success" Speech, 1930

The mass collectivization attempt of 1929 turned out to be disastrous, despite what the Central Committee may have reported (see previous excerpt). The peasants had slaughtered their livestock to protest collectivization, which destroyed the draft power and fertilizer needed to maintain the farms. Leaders of the collective farms used violence to force peasants to join and they falsified reports of success. The economic situation was worsening. So, in March 1930, Stalin gave his famous "Dizzy with Success" speech, excerpted here. Despite these failures, how does Stalin still see collectivization as a success? In particular, how does he believe collectivization solved the age-old "peasant question" for the Communist Party? Who does Stalin blame for the failures of the collectivization plan, and what solutions does he offer? What are the implications of this piece?

Everybody is now talking about the successes achieved by the Soviet government in the sphere of the collective-farm movement. Even our enemies are compelled to admit that important successes have been achieved. And these successes are great indeed.

It is a fact that by February 20, this year, 50 percent of the peasant farms of the, USSR had been collectivized. This means that by February 20, 1930, we had fulfilled the estimates of the Five-Year Plan more than twice over.

It is a fact that by February 28, this year, the collective farms had already stored more than 600,000 tons of seed for the spring sowing, i.e., more than 90 percent of the plan, or about 220,000,000 poods. It cannot but be admitted that the storing of 220,000,000 poods of seed by the collective farms alone, after the grain-purchasing plan had been successfully fulfilled, is a tremendous achievement.

What does all this show?

It shows that the radical turn of the rural districts towards Socialism may already be regarded as guaranteed.

There is no need to prove that these successes are of tremendous importance for the fate of our country, for the whole working class as the leading force of our country, and, finally, for the Party itself. Apart from the direct practical results, these successes are of tremendous importance for the internal life of the Party itself, for the education of our Party. They imbue the Party with a spirit of cheerfulness and confidence in its strength. They arm the working class with confidence in the triumph of our cause. They bring to our Party new millions of reserves.

But successes also have their seamy side; especially when they are achieved with comparative "ease," "unexpectedly," so to speak. Such successes sometimes induce a spirit of conceit and arrogance. "We can do anything!" "We can win hands down!" People are often intoxicated by such successes, they become dizzy with success, they lose all sense of proportion, they lose the faculty of understanding realities, they reveal a tendency to overestimate their own strength and to underestimate the strength of the enemy; reckless attempts are made to settle all the problems of Socialist construction "in two ticks."

... Hence the task of the Party: to wage a determined struggle against this frame of mind, which is dangerous and harmful to the cause, and to drive it out of the Party.

A few facts:

1. The success of our collective farm policy is due, among other things, to the fact that this policy rests on the voluntary character of the collective-farm movement, and that it allows for the diversity of conditions existing in the various parts of the USSR. Collective farms cannot be set up by force. To do so would be stupid and reactionary. The collective-farm movement must rely on the active support of the great bulk of the peasantry. Methods of collective farm construction in developed districts cannot be mechanically transplanted to backward districts ... .

But what really happens sometimes? Can it be said that the voluntary principle and the principle of allowing for local peculiarities are not violated in a number of districts? No, unfortunately, that cannot be said ... Take certain districts in Turkestan, where there are fewer favorable conditions for the immediate organization of collective farms than in the northern regions of the grain-importing belt. We know that in a number of districts in Turkestan attempts have already been made to "overtake and outstrip" the advanced districts of the USSR by the method of threatening to military force, by the method of threatening to deprive the peasants who do not as yet want to join the collective farms of irrigation water and of manufactured goods.

Original Source: *Pravda,* 2 March 1930. Also in: I. V. Stalin, *Problems of Leninism*. Moscow: Foreign Language Publishers, 1934.

READING 56

Letter to Stalin and Mikhail Kalinin from Workers at the Red Putilovets Factory, Leningrad, 1930

The "Dizzy with Success" speech (see above) did not stop the process of collectivization; it only slowed it down. What followed between 1931 and 1933 was a terrible famine in the grain producing regions of the Soviet Union, particularly Ukraine and Kazakhstan. This event is known by historians as the *Holodomor* in Ukraine and the Goloshchekin in Kazakhstan. There is significant disagreement among scholars over the causes of the famine. There is evidence that bad weather played a role in hurting crops, but there can be no denying that the Soviet state was complicit in allowing an estimated six to eight million Ukrainians and Kazakhs starve to death in these terrible years. Authorities kept up their grain collections, knowing that there were no reserves left in the countryside. They blocked news of the famine from reaching the outside world and refused aid. Amidst all of this, there did exist significant resistance to collectivization, not just in the countryside, but in the urban factories. In this piece, ask yourself who the people are that are writing this letter to Stalin? What are they protesting and why? What is the distinction between the worker and the peasant in this letter, and how does it differ from the Party's understanding of that distinction?

(*The grammatical and spelling errors here are copied from the original*) We, the workers of the Red Putilovets plant, fiftey in number, have discussed and have decided that we once and for all protest against the terors and persecutions of the peasants and the ones who you deprive of the vote and consider them kulaks. We all as one, members of the VKPb All Union Communist Party of the Soviet Union have a tie with the countryside, to us write our fathers and brothers how they're deprived of the vote and are not asked if they are agreed to be on the kolkhoz or not, but right off the bat their property is taken by the careerists, and they're driven into prisons the shame of Soviet power, as capitalists do not do as you do in a free country, you throw into prison those who worked from morning till late night, the toilers who've put their whole life into their home and into their farm. You've called them kulaks only because they slept on their fist not having a pillow to themselves in their home. You regard those as kulaks who made their farm prosper and gave income to the state. You drove them into cellars and want them to rot alive, these fathers and brothers of ours, and posted their grandson with a rifle to guard them like wild animals. We're indignant against this, for what have we fought, for what have we shed blood when we did not expect this, that our worker-peasant reign would torment our fathers and brothers so. Why then do we need the VKP since it makes life impossible for all of us?

Source: State Archive of the Russian Federation (GARF), f. 1235., op. 4, d. 47, ll. 164–165. Taken from Siegelbaum, Lewis and Andrei Sokolov, eds. *Stalinism as a Way of Life*. New Haven: Yale University Press, 2000.

READING 57

Excerpt from Vasily Grossman, *Everything Flows*, 1970

This is a short excerpt from the seminal book, *Everything Flows*, which was written by one of the Soviet Union's most famous authors, Vasily Grossman. In it, he describes the destruction wrought by dekulakization and collectivization. What world is he describing here? How does this recounting differ from the Soviet State's explanation for these events?

During the autumn people took to living on potatoes—but without bread, it doesn't take long to get through potatoes. Toward Christmas they began slaughtering their cattle … . they slaughtered the chickens, of course. Soon they'd got through all their meat. And there wasn't so much as a drop of milk to be found in the village. Nor was there a single egg. And worst of all, there was no grain, no bread. Every last kernel had been requisitioned. Come spring, there would be no spring wheat to sow, the entire seed fund had gone … .

It was terrible. Mothers looked at their own children—and screamed in fear. It was as if they'd seen a snake in the house. And they had seen a snake; they had seen famine, starvation, death.

Source: Grossman, Vasily. *Everything Flows*. Translated by Robert Chandler. New York: New York Review of Books, 2009.

READING 58

Report of the All-Union Resettlement Committee on Resettling Collective Farmers to Ukraine (with Table), 1933

Can you make sense of this short report? Look at who wrote it and to whom it was written. This was written at the end of 1933 after the *Holodomor* in Ukraine had mostly ended. What populations are being moved and where (feel free to get a map)? Why were they moving? What do you think the word "echelons" means in this context? What is the sad significance of this seemingly business-like report?

DECEMBER 29, 1933
EXPRESS. SECRET

To Head of GULAG OGPU Comrade Berman,

The All-Union Resettlement Committee of the SNK USSR is sending operational report No. 38 on resettlement to Ukraine as of December 28 this year … . In total 21,856 collective farms, 117,149 persons, 14,879 horses, 21,898 cows and 38,705 heads of other livestock (the latter includes only swine and sheep) have been relocated. The report is attached.

Deputy Chairman, All-Union Resettlement Committee,

SUMMARY DATA ON ECHELONS OF RESETTLERS SENT TO UKRAINE AS OF DECEMBER 28, 1933

SOURCE OBLAST	DESTINATION OBLAST	HOUSEHOLDS	HORSES	COWS	OTHER LIVESTOCK	ECHELONS	% PLAN COMPLETION
Gorky	Odesa	2,120	1,348	2,062	2,050	35	106
Ivanov	Donetsk	3,527	1,619	3,498	1,980	44	104
BSSR	Odesa	4,630	3,864	5,295	10,924	61	103
C.Chornozem	Kharkiv	4,800	2,329	3,472	5,644	80	106.6
Western	Dnipropetrovsk	6,679	5,719	7,571	18,097	109	102.7

1. On 28 December 1933, 329 echelons were dispatched, 21,856 households, 117,149 family members, 14,879 horses, 21,898 cows and 38,705 heads of small livestock.
2. The plan for transporting collective farmers into Ukraine is complete and fulfilled by 104.7%.

Deputy chairman, All Union Resettlement Committee,

USSR SNK Rud'

Source: Report of the All-Union Resettlement Committee on resettling collective farmers to Ukraine (with table), RGAE, fond 5675, opis 1, delo 33, list 56, cited in *Collectivization and famine in Ukraine: 1929–1933*. Kyiv: Holovne arkhivne upravlinnia, 1992.

READING 59

Stalin's Speech at the First All-Union Conference of Stakhanovites, 1935

The 1930s also witnessed an explosive rise in industrial output in the Soviet Union. While the rest of the world was suffering under the weight of the Great Depression, the Soviet Union experienced growth rates that were unprecedented in its history. There are still no reliable statistics on the rate of growth. What we do know is that industrialization changed the Russian political and cultural landscape. One of the most fascinating products of this industrialization was the rise of the Stakhanov movement. It was named after a coal miner, Alexei Stakhanov, who exceeded his production quota fourteen times over by reportedly mining a record 102 tons of coal in one shift in 1935. Workers who set production records or showed mastery in a skill were labelled Stakhanovites. They became models for what the "new Soviet man" was capable of achieving. What significances does Stalin give to the Stakhanov movement? How does Stalin see the Stakhanov movement as a vehicle for the rise of Communism? What is the "antithesis between mental and physical labor," and how does the Stakhanov movement (and the Soviet project) promise to fix it?

Wherein lies the significance of the Stakhanov movement? ... .

The Stakhanov movement is a movement of working men and women which sets itself the aim of surpassing the present technical standards, surpassing the existing designed capacities, surpassing the existing production plans and estimates. Surpassing them—because these standards have already become antiquated for our day, for our new people. This movement is breaking down the old views on technique, it is shattering the old technical standards, the old designed capacities, and the old production plans, and demands the creation of new and higher technical standards, design capacities, and production plans. It is destined to produce a revolution in our industry. That is why the Stakhanov movement is at bottom a profoundly revolutionary movement.

It has already been said here that the Stakhanov movement, as an expression of new and higher technical standards, is a model of that high productivity of labor which only socialism can give, and which capitalism cannot give. That is absolutely true. Why was it that capitalism smashed and defeated feudalism? Because it created higher standards of productivity of labor, it enabled society to procure an incomparably greater quantity of products than could be procured under the feudal system; because it made society richer. Why is it that socialism can, should, and certainly will defeat the capitalist system of economy? Because it can furnish higher models of labor, a higher productivity of labor, than the capitalist system of economy; because it can provide society with more products and can make society richer than the capitalist system of economy.

Some people think that socialism can be consolidated by a certain equalization of people's material conditions, based on a poor man's standard of living. That is not true. That is a petty-bourgeois conception of socialism. In point of fact, socialism can succeed only on the basis of a high productivity of labor, higher than under capitalism, on the basis of an abundance of products and of articles of consumption of all kinds, on the basis of a prosperous and cultured life for all members of society. But if socialism is to achieve this aim and make our Soviet society the most prosperous of all societies, our country must have a productivity of labor which surpasses that of the foremost capitalist countries. Without this we cannot even think of securing an abundance of products and of articles of consumption of all kinds ... .

But the significance of the Stakhanov movement does not end there. Its significance lies also in the fact that it is preparing the conditions for the transition from socialism to communism.

The principle of socialism is that in a socialist society each works according to his ability and receives articles of consumption, not according to his needs, but according to the work he performs for society. This means that the cultural and technical level of the working class is as yet not a high one, that the antithesis between mental and physical labor still exists, that the productivity of labor is still not high enough to ensure an abundance of articles of consumption, and, as a result, society is obliged to distribute articles of consumption not in accordance with the needs of its members, but in accordance with the work they perform for society.

Communism represents a higher stage of development. The principle of communism is that in a communist society each works according to his abilities and receives articles of consumption, not according to the work he performs, but according to his needs as a culturally developed individual. This means that the cultural and technical level of the working class has become high enough to undermine the basis of the antithesis between mental labor and physical labor, that the antithesis between mental labor and physical labor has already disappeared, and that productivity of labor has reached such a high level that it can provide an absolute abundance of articles of consumption, and as a result society is able to distribute these articles in accordance with the needs of its members.

Some people think that the elimination of the antithesis between mental labor and physical labor can be achieved by means of a certain cultural and technical equalization of mental and manual workers by lowering the cultural and technical level of engineers and technicians, of mental workers, to the level of average skilled workers. That is absolutely incorrect. Only petty-bourgeois windbags can conceive communism in this way. In reality the elimination of the antithesis between mental labor and physical labor can be brought about only by raising the cultural and technical level of the working class to the level of engineers and technical workers. It would be absurd to think that this is unfeasible. It is entirely feasible under the Soviet system, where the productive forces of the country have been freed from the fetters of capitalism, where labor has been freed from the yoke of exploitation, where the working class is in power, and where the younger generation of the working class has every opportunity of obtaining an adequate technical education. There is no reason to doubt that only such a rise in the cultural and technical level of the working class can undermine the basis of the antithesis between mental labor and physical labor, that only this can ensure the high level of productivity of labor and the abundance of articles of consumption which are necessary in order to begin the transition from socialism to communism.

Source: Various Authors. *Labour in the Land of Socialism: Stakhanovites in Conference* Moscow: Cooperative Publishing Society of Foreign Workers in the U. S. S. R., 1937.

READING 60

Maxim Gorky's Speech on Soviet Literature (and Socialist Realism), 1934

The transformations of the 1930s were not reserved for just agriculture and industry. The Soviet leadership believed that the arts had to change as well. In 1934, at the Soviet Writers' Congress, four guidelines were laid out for the creation of art, film, and literature. These became the foundations of a new kind of cultural production called "Socialist Realism." The four guidelines were that works must be (1) Proletarian: meaningful and understandable by the workers, (2) Typical: depicting scenes of everyday life, (3) Realistic: representational and easy to decipher, without abstract subjectivity or images that were hard to understand, and (4) Partisan: promoting the goals of the State and the Party. Below is an excerpt of Maxim Gorky's famous speech where he introduces the idea of Socialist Realism. How does he define it? Can you see what the potential problems might be for this artistic movement? Do a search for some Socialist Realist art. Is it good? What role is it performing? Have you seen this kind of art anywhere else or is this just a Soviet phenomenon?

Life, as asserted by socialist realism, is deeds, creativeness, the aim of which is the uninterrupted development of the priceless individual faculties of man, with a view to his victory over the forces of nature, for the sake of his health and longevity, for the supreme joy of living on an earth which, in conformity with the steady growth of his requirements, he wishes to mold throughout into a beautiful dwelling place for mankind, united into a single family ... .

The proletarian state must educate thousands of first class "craftsmen of culture," "engineers of the soul." This is necessary in order to restore to the whole mass of the working people the right to develop their intelligence, talents and faculties—a right of which they have been deprived everywhere else in the world. This aim, which is a fully practicable one, imposes on us writers the need of strict responsibility for our work and our social behavior. This places us not only in the position, traditional to realist literature, of "judges of the world and men," "critics of life," but gives us the right to participate directly in the construction of a new life, in the process of "changing the world." The possession of this right should impress every writer with a sense of his duty and responsibility for all literature.

The Union of Soviet Writers unites 1,500 persons. In ratio to the total population, we thus have one writer to every hundred thousand readers. This is not much; the inhabitants of the Scandinavian peninsula at the beginning of this century had one writer to every 230 readers. The population of the Union of Socialist Republics is constantly and almost daily demonstrating its giftedness, but we should not think that we shall soon have 1,500 writers of genius. Let us hope for fifty. Not to be deceived, let us say five writers of genius and forty-five very talented ones. I think this figure will do for a start. In the balance, we get people who are still insufficiently attentive to realities, who organize their material poorly or work on it carelessly. To this balance should be added the many hundreds of candidates to the union, and further, hundreds of "beginners" in all the republics and regions.

Source: Gorky, Maxim. *Soviet Writers' Congress, 1934: The Debate on Socialist Realism and Modernism*. Translated by Jose Braz. New York: Lawrence & Wishart, 1977.

READING 61

Materials on the Kirov Murder, 1934–1990, Prepared by a TSK KPSS Commission, 1961

The murder of Sergei Kirov was the spark that began Stalin's Great Terror of the late 1930s. Between 1936 and 1938, upwards of two million people were arrested and either shot or sent to the GULAG for suspected conspiratorial crimes against Stalin and the Soviet State. A third of the members of the Communist Party in the Soviet Union were arrested. Only two people from the original 1924 Politburo survived: Stalin and Trotsky. Eighty percent of the 1934 Central Committee were executed or driven to suicide before they could be arrested and shot. In many of these cases, people were accused of having first participated in the conspiracy to assassinate Sergei Kirov. It is now commonly believed that Stalin orchestrated Kirov's assassination in order to have an excuse to start the Terror. The excerpt below is taken from a 1961 report where the KGB reexamined the real causes of Kirov's murder. What conclusions does it draw? What observations does it still choose not to make here?

CONCERNING THE RESULTS OF THE EXAMINATION OF MATERIALS OF THE COURT PROCEEDINGS IN THE CASE OF S. M. KIROV'S MURDER

[This is the *KGB* report completed in 1961.]

On December 1, 1934, at 1630 hours in the City of Leningrad, in the headquarters of the *oblast'* committee of the All-Union Communist Party (Bolshevik) [*VKP(b)*], in the third floor corridor, a shot from a revolver killed S. M. Kirov, a member of the Presidium of the Central Executive Committee of the USSR and the Secretary of the Central Committee and the Leningrad *Oblast'* Committee of the *VKP(b)*. The foul murder of S. M. Kirov was committed by one Nikolaev L. V., who was arrested at the scene of the crime.

The following persons were arrested in connection with this terrorist act in December 1934 and were bound over for trial as members of an underground counterrevolutionary terrorist group responsible for arranging S. M. Kirov's murder: Nikolaev L. V., Kotolynov I. I., Shatskii N. N.,

Rumiantsev V. V., Mandel'shtam S. O., Miasnikov N. P., Levin V. S., Sositskii L. I., Sokolov G. V., IUskin I. G., Zvezdov V. I., Antonov N. S., Khanik L. O., and Tolmazov A. I., a total of 14 individuals.

On December 28 and 29 the case against Nikolaev and the others was heard by the Leningrad Military Collegium of the Supreme Court of the USSR following a streamlined procedure, without calling any witnesses and without a prosecutor or defense attorney.

In its verdict the court stated that in 1933–1934 in Leningrad, an underground terrorist group consisting of former members of the Zinovievite opposition was organized and operated under the direction of a "Leningrad Center," consisting of Levin, Rumiantsev, Kotolynov, Mandel'shtam, Miasnikov, Sositskii, Shatskii, and Nikolaev. This center planned and organized the murder of S. M. Kirov. Under the direct supervision of Kotolynov and with the active cooperation of Shatskii, IUskin, Sokolov, Antonov, Zvezdov, Tolmazov, and Khanik, after lengthy preparations, Nikolaev, under the direct orders of the "Leningrad Center," murdered S. M. Kirov.

The court also determined that the leaders of this terrorist group were hoping for an armed intervention by foreign countries and that for this purpose Nikolaev, on Kotolynov's suggestion, had established criminal relations with Biseneks, the Latvian consul in Leningrad, in September 1934.

The Military Collegium of the Supreme Court of the USSR found all the defendants guilty of participating in the commission of a terrorist act (Article 58-8 of the Criminal Code of the Russian Soviet Federated Socialist Republic (RSFSR)) and being members of an anti-Soviet organization (Article 58-11 of the Criminal Code of the RSFSR) and sentenced them to death by shooting and confiscation of all their personal property. The sentence was not subject to appeal and was executed the very same day, December 29, 1934.

RECOMMENDATIONS

I. In light of the blatant fabrications and obvious flaws in the accusations that Kotolynov, Shatskii, Rumiantsev, Mandel'shtam, Miasnikov, Sositskii, Levin, Antonov, Khanik, Tolmazov, Sokolov, IUskin, and Zvezdov took part in organizing a so-called underground, terrorist, Zinovievite organization headed by the "Leningrad Center," which in reality never existed, and the total lack of involvement of these individuals in preparing and committing the terrorist act against S. M. Kirov, we deem it necessary to invalidate the verdicts against these individuals and close the case against them due to a lack of the elements of a crime in their actions.

Source: Koenker, Diane and Ronald Bachman eds., *Revelations from the Russian Archives*. Washington, D.C.: Library of Congress, 1997.

READING 62

The Moscow Show Trials, 1936-38

The most famous conspiracy cases of the Great Terror became great show trials that were broadcast for the entire nation to hear in the late 1930s. This is an excerpt from the trial of Lev Kamenev and Grigory Zinoviev, who were original members of the Bolshevik Party, close friends of Lenin, and two of the core organizers of the 1917 Revolution. They had been in opposition to Stalin for over a decade at this point, and were accused of conspiring to kill Kirov, Stalin, and many others along with collaborating with foreign enemies. As you read, think about the language that the prosecuting lawyer, Andrei Vyshinsky, uses to condemn these men. How does he describe them? What accusations does he levy against them? How might you have understood this if you had not known what we know now?

The enemy throws new forces to the front without regard to heavy losses and penetrates deep into the Soviet Union, seizing new regions, destroying our cities and villages, and violating, plundering and killing the Soviet population. Combat goes on in region Voronej, near Don, in the south, and at the gates of the Northern Caucasus. The German invaders penetrate toward Stalingrad, to Volga and want at any cost to trap Kuban and the Northern Caucasus, with their oil and grain. The enemy already has captured Vorochilovgrad, Starobelsk, Rossosh, Kupyansk, Valuyki, Novochercassk, Rostov on Don, half Voronej. Part of the troops of the Southern front, following the panic-mongers, have left Rostov and Novochercassk without severe resistance and without orders from Moscow, covering their banners with shame.

The population of our country, who love and respect the Red Army, start to be discouraged in her, and lose faith in the Red Army, and many curse the Red Army for leaving our people under the yoke of the German oppressors, and itself running east.

Some stupid people at the front calm themselves with talk that we can retreat further to the east, as we have a lot of territory, a lot of ground, a lot of population and that there will always be much bread for us.

They want to justify the infamous behavior at the front. But such talk is falsehood, helpful only to our enemies.

Each commander, Red Army soldier and political commissar should understand that our means are not limitless. The territory of the Soviet state is not a desert, but people - workers, peasants, intelligentsia, our fathers, mothers, wives, brothers, children. The territory of the USSR which the enemy has captured and aims to capture is bread and other products for the army, metal and fuel for industry, factories, plants supplying the army with arms and ammunition, railroads. After the loss of Ukraine, Belarus, Baltic republics, Donetzk, and other areas we have much less territory, much less people, bread, metal, plants and factories. We have lost more than 70 million people, more than 800 million pounds of bread annually and more than 10 million tons of metal annually. Now we do not have predominance over the Germans in human reserves, in reserves of bread. To retreat further - means to waste ourselves and to waste at the same time our Motherland.

Therefore it is necessary to eliminate talk that we have the capability endlessly to retreat, that we have a lot of territory, that our country is great and rich, that there is a large population, and that bread always will be abundant. Such talk is false and parasitic, it weakens us and benefits the enemy, if we do not stop retreating we will be without bread, without fuel, without metal, without raw material, without factories and plants, without railroads.

This leads to the conclusion, it is time to finish retreating.

Not one step back! Such should now be our main slogan.

It is necessary to defend each position, each meter of our territory, up to the last drop of blood, to cling for each plot of Soviet land and to defend it as long as possible.

Our Motherland is experiencing hard days. We must stop, and then to throw back and smash the enemy regardless of cost. The Germans are not so strong, as it seems to the panic-mongers. They strain their last forces. To withstand their impact now, means to ensure our victory in some months.

Can we withstand the impact, and then throw back the enemy to the west? Yes we can, because our factories and plants in the rear are fine and our army receives ever more and more airplanes, tanks, artillery and mortars.

What do we lack?

There is no order and discipline in companies, battalions, regiments, in tank units and air squadrons. This is our main deficiency. We should establish in our army the most stringent order and solid discipline, if we want to salvage the situation, and to keep our Motherland.

It is impossible to tolerate commanders and commissars permitting units to leave their positions. It is impossible to tolerate commanders and commissars who admit that some panic-mongers determined the situation on the field of combat and carried away in departure other soldiers and opened the front to the enemy.

The panic-mongers and cowards should be exterminated in place.

Henceforth the solid law of discipline for each commander, Red Army soldier, and commissar should be the requirement - not a single step back without order from higher command. Company, battalion, regiment and division - commanders and appropriate commissars, who retreat without orders from higher commanders, are betrayers of the Motherland.

These are the orders of our Motherland.

To execute this order - means to defend our lands, to save the Motherland, to exterminate and to conquer the hated enemy.

After the winter retreat under pressure of the Red Army, when in German troops discipline became loose, the Germans for recovery of discipline imposed severe measures which resulted in quite good outcomes. They formed 100 penal companies from soldiers who were guilty of breaches of discipline because of cowardice or bewilderment, put them at dangerous sections of the front and commanded them to redeem their sins by blood. They have also formed approximately ten penal battalions from commanders guilty of breaches of discipline through cowardice or bewilderment, deprived them of their decorations, transferred them to even more dangerous sections of the front and commanded them to redeem their sins. Finally, they have formed special squads and put them behind unstable divisions and ordered them to shoot panic-mongers in case of unauthorized retreats or attempted surrender. As we know, these measures were effective, and now German troops fight better than they fought in the winter. And here is the situation, that the German troops have good discipline, though they do not have the high purpose of protection of the Motherland, and have only one extortionate purpose - to subdue another's country, and our troops have the higher purpose of protecting the abused Motherland, and do not have such discipline and so suffer defeat. Is it necessary for us to learn from our enemies, as our grandparents studied their enemies in the past and achieved victory?

I think it is necessary.

The Supreme General Headquarters of the Red Army commands:

1. Military councils of the fronts and first of all front commanders should:
   a. Unconditionally eliminate retreat moods in the troops and with a firm hand bar propaganda that we can and should retreat further east, and that such retreat will cause no harm;
   b. Unconditionally remove from their posts and send to the High Command for court martial those army commanders who have allowed unauthorized troop withdrawals from occupied positions, without the order of the Front command.
   c. Form within each Front from one up to three (depending on the situation) penal battalions (800 persons) where commanders and high commanders and appropriate commissars of all service arms who have been guilty of a breach of discipline due to cowardice or bewilderment will be sent, and put them on more difficult sectors of the front to give them an opportunity to redeem by blood their crimes against the Motherland.

2. Military councils of armies and first of all army commanders should;
   a. Unconditionally remove from their offices corps and army commanders and commissars who have accepted troop withdrawals from occupied positions without the order of the army command, and route them to the military councils of the fronts for court martial;
   b. Form within the limits of each army 3 to 5 well-armed defensive squads (up to 200 persons in each), and put them directly behind unstable divisions and require them in case of panic and scattered withdrawals of elements of the divisions to shoot in place panic-mongers and cowards and thus help the honest soldiers of the division execute their duty to the Motherland;
   c. Form within the limits of each army up to ten (depending on the situation) penal companies (from 150 to 200 persons in each) where ordinary soldiers and low ranking commanders who have been guilty of a breach of discipline due to cowardice or bewilderment will be routed, and put them at difficult sectors of the army to give them an opportunity to redeem by blood their crimes against the Motherland.

3. Commanders and commissars of corps and divisions should;
   a. Unconditionally remove from their posts commanders and commissars of regiments and battalions who have accepted unwarranted withdrawal of their troops without the order of the corps or division commander, take from them their orders and medals and route them to military councils of fronts for court martial;

b. Render all help and support to the defensive squads of the army in their business of strengthening order and discipline in the units.

This order is to be read in all companies, cavalry squadrons, batteries, squadrons, commands and headquarters.

People's commissar for defense of the USSR: J. Stalin.

Source: People's Commissariat of Justice of the U.S.S.R. *Report of Court Proceedings, The Case of the Trotskyite-Zinovievite Terrorist Centre*. Translated by Brian Biggins. Moscow: Partizdat, 1936.

chapter
EIGHT

USSR in the Great Patriotic War,
Cold War, and Reconstruction

READING 63

Adolf Hitler's "Directive for the Treatment of Political Commissars" (Commissar Order), 1941

On June 6, 1941, Hitler issued this directive to be distributed to the German Commanders-in-Chief of the Army and Navy. In it, he made clear his intention for how Soviet commissars should be handled. Do some outside research to find out who commissars were. Why did Hitler want them eradicated, in particular? What does he mean when he speaks of international law and the Hague Convention? What is the larger significance of this order given that the Molotov-Ribbentrop Pact was still in effect?

The war against Russia cannot be fought in knightly fashion. The struggle is one of ideologies and racial differences and will have to be waged with unprecedented, unmerciful, and unrelenting hardness. All officers will have to get rid of any old fashioned ideas they may have. I realize that the necessity for conducting such warfare is beyond the comprehension of you generals, but I must insist that my orders be followed without complaint. The commissars hold views directly opposite to those of National Socialism. Hence these commissars must be eliminated. Any German soldier who breaks international law will be pardoned. Russia did not take part in the Hague Convention and, therefore, has no rights under it.

Source: High Command of the German Armed forces. *Directives for the Treatment of Political Commissars*. June 6, 1941. *German History in Documents and Images*. Berlin: GHDI, 2017. Vol. 7, 1933–1945.

READING 64

Molotov's Radio Broadcast Announcing War with Germany, 1941

This speech is considered by many to be one of the greatest calls-to-arms of the twentieth century. And yet, the truth is that it was delivered on the fly by a leadership that was in chaos. Because the Soviets had not prepared for the Nazi invasion, one quarter of Russia's air strength was destroyed in the first day and thousands of Red Army soldiers were killed or taken prisoner. This speech rallied the Soviet people, nonetheless. In the four years to come, the Soviet Union would sacrifice an estimated 24 million to the cause of defeating the Nazis. As you read this speech, think about the language that Molotov uses to rally his people. What points does Molotov make? How does history serve to reassure the Soviet people about its odds against the Germans?

CITIZENS OF THE SOVIET UNION

The Soviet Government and its head, Comrade Stalin, have authorized me to make the following statement:

Today at 4 o'clock A.M., without any claims having been presented to the Soviet Union, without a declaration of war, German troops attacked our country, attacked our borders at many points and bombed from their airplanes our cities Zhitomir, Kiev, Sebastopol, Kaunas and some others, killing and wounding over 200 persons.

There were also enemy air raids and artillery shelling from Rumanian and Finnish territory.

This unheard of attack upon our country is perfidy unparalleled in the history of civilized nations. The attack on our country was perpetrated despite the fact that a treaty of non-aggression had been signed between the U.S.S.R. and Germany and that the Soviet Government most faithfully abided by all provisions of this treaty.

The attack upon our country was perpetrated despite the fact that during the entire period of operation of this treaty the German Government could not find grounds for a single complaint against the U.S.S.R. as regards observance of this treaty.

Entire responsibility for this predatory attack upon the Soviet Union falls fully and completely upon the German Fascist rulers.

At 5:30 A.M.—that is, after the attack had already been perpetrated, Von der Schulenburg, the German Ambassador in Moscow, on behalf of his government made the statement to me as People's Commissar of Foreign Affairs to the effect that the German Government had decided to launch war against the U.S.S.R. in connection with the concentration of Red Army units near the eastern German frontier.

In reply to this I stated on behalf of the Soviet Government that, until the very last moment, the German Government had not presented any claims to the Soviet Government that Germany attacked the U.S.S.R. despite the peaceable position of the Soviet Union, and that for this reason Fascist Germany is the aggressor.

On instruction of the government of the Soviet Union I also stated that at no point had our troops or our air force committed a violation of the frontier and therefore the statement made this morning by the Rumanian radio to the effect that Soviet aircraft allegedly had fired on Rumanian airdromes is a sheer lie and provocation.

Likewise a lie and provocation is the whole declaration made today by Hitler, who is trying belatedly to concoct accusations charging the Soviet Union with failure to observe the Soviet-German pact.

Now that the attack on the Soviet Union has already been committed, the Soviet Government has ordered our troops to repulse the predatory assault and drive German troops from the territory of our country.

This war has been forced upon us, not by the German people, not by German workers, peasants and intellectuals, whose sufferings we well understand, but by the clique of bloodthirsty Fascist rulers of Germany who have enslaved Frenchmen, Czechs, Poles, Serbians, Norway, Belgium, Denmark, Holland, Greece and other nations.

The government of the Soviet Union expresses its unshakable confidence that our valiant army and navy and brave falcons of the Soviet Air Force will acquit themselves with honor in performing their duty to the fatherland and to the Soviet people, and will inflict a crushing blow upon the aggressor.

This is not the first time that our people have had to deal with an attack of an arrogant foe. At the time of Napoleon's invasion of Russia our people's reply was war for the fatherland, and Napoleon suffered defeat and met his doom.

It will be the same with Hitler, who in his arrogance has proclaimed a new crusade against our country. The Red Army and our whole people will again wage victorious war for the fatherland, for our country, for honor, for liberty.

The government of the Soviet Union expresses the firm conviction that the whole population of our country, all workers, peasants and intellectuals, men and women, will conscientiously perform their duties and do their work. Our entire people must now stand solid and united as never before.

Each one of us must demand of himself and of others discipline, organization and self-denial worthy of real Soviet patriots, in order to provide for all the needs of the Red Army, Navy and Air Force, to insure victory over the enemy.

The government calls upon you, citizens of the Soviet Union to rally still more closely around our glorious Bolshevist party around our Soviet government, around our great leader and comrade, Stalin. Ours is a righteous cause. The enemy shall be defeated. Victory will be ours.

Source: Molotov, Vyacheslav M. "The Nazi War on Russia," *The World's Great Speeches*. Edited and translated by Lewis Copeland, Lawrence H. Lamm, and Stephen J. McKenna. London: Dover Publications, 1999. Copyright © 1999 by Dover Publications. Reprinted with permission.

READING 65

Testimony of Dina Pronicheva on the Babi Yar Massacre, 1941

Between September 29–30, the Nazis killed 33,771 Jews living in Kiev, Ukraine. Babi Yar is the ravine where the massacre took place. It has become one of the lasting symbols of Nazi and Ukrainian-collaborationist barbarity during the Holocaust. The scale and horror of it is incomprehensible. What does it mean to remember this? What responsibility do the living have to attend to these stories?

Before the war I was an actress at the Kiev Young Viewers' Theater. My husband left for the front on the second day of the war and I was left with our small children and a sick old mother. Hitler's troops occupied Kiev on September 19, 1941 and from the very first day started to rob and kill Jews. … . We were living in terror. When I saw the posters on the city's streets and read the order: "All the Jews of Kiev must gather at Babi Yar," about which we had no idea, in my heart I sensed trouble. A tremor shook my entire body. I understood that nothing good was awaiting us at Babi Yar. So I dressed my little ones, the younger one [the girl] who was 3 years old and the older one [the boy]— 5, packed their belongings into a small sack, and took my daughter and son to my Russian mother-in-law. Afterwards, I took my sick mother and, following the order, she and I started out on the way to Babi Yar.

Hundreds, no thousands, of Jews were walking the same way. An old Jew with a long white beard walked next to me. He wore a talis [prayer shawl] and tefillin [phylacteries]. He was murmuring quietly. He prayed the same way as my father did when I was a child. Ahead of me a woman with two children in her arms walked along, while the third child clung to her apron-strings. The sick women and elderly people were taken by carts, on which bags and suitcases were piled up. Small children were crying. The older people who had difficulty walking were sighing in a barely audible way, but they silently continued their path of sorrow … .

Russian husbands accompanied their Jewish wives.

Russian wives accompanied their Jewish husbands.

When we neared Babi Yar, shooting and inhuman cries could be heard. I started to grasp what was going on, but said nothing to my mother … .

Each time I saw a new group of men and women, elderly people, and children being forced to take off their clothes. All [of them] were being taken to an open pit where submachine-gunners shot them. Then another group was brought … .

With my own eyes I saw this horror. Although I was not standing close to the pit, terrible cries of panic-stricken people and children's voices calling "Mother, mother …" reached me.

I saw all this, but in no way could I understand how people were killing other human beings only because they were Jews. And then I understood that Fascists are not human beings, but beasts. … I saw a young woman, completely naked, nursing her naked baby when a policeman came running up to her, tore the baby from her breast, and threw it into the pit alive. The mother rushed there after her baby. The fascist shot her and she fell down dead … .

The policeman ordered me to strip and pushed me to a precipice, where another group of people was awaiting their fate. But before the shots resounded, apparently out of fear, I fell into the pit. I fell on the [bodies] of those already murdered … . During the first moments I couldn't grasp anything—either where I was or how I got there.

I thought that I had gone mad, but when people started to fall on top of me, I regained consciousness and understood everything. I started to feel my arms, legs, stomach, [and] head to make certain that I had not even been wounded.

I pretended to be dead. Those who had been killed or wounded were lying under me and on top of me—many were still breathing, others were moaning … . Suddenly I heard a child weeping and the cry: "Mummy!" I imagined my little girl crying and I started to cry myself.

The shooting was continuing and people kept falling. I threw bodies off of me, afraid of being buried alive. I did so in a way that would not attract the attention of the policemen.

Suddenly all became quiet. It was getting dark. Germans armed with submachine-guns walked around, finishing off the wounded. I felt that somebody was standing above me, but I did not give any sign that I was alive, even though that was very difficult. Then I felt we were being covered with earth. I closed my eyes so that the soil would not get into them, and when it became dark and silent, literally the silence of death, I opened my eyes and threw the sand off me, making sure that no one was close by, no one was around, no one was watching me. I saw the pit with thousands of dead bodies. I was overcome by terror. In some places the earth was heaving—people half-alive were [still] breathing.

I looked at myself and was terror stricken—the undershirt covering my naked body was soaked with blood. I tried to stand up but was unable to do so. Then I said to myself: "Dina, stand up. Get away. Run from here, your children are waiting for you." So I stood up and ran, but then I heard a shot and understood that I had been seen. I fell to the ground and remained silent. It was quiet. Still on the ground, I started to move quietly toward the high hill[s] surrounding the pit. Suddenly I felt that something was moving behind me. At first I was afraid and decided to wait for a minute. I turned around quietly and asked: "Who are you?"

I was answered by a thin, scared child's voice: "Auntie, don't be afraid, it's me. My name is Fima. My last name is Shnaiderman. I am 11 years old. Take me with you. I am very afraid of the dark."

I moved closer to the boy, hugged him tightly, and started to weep silently. The boy said: "Don't cry, Auntie."

We both started to move silently. We reached the edge of the precipice, rested a little, and then continued to climb further, helping each other. We had reached the top of the pit and were standing, about to proceed in the direction we thought best, when a shot rang out. By instinct we both fell to the ground. We kept silent for several minutes, afraid to utter a single word. When I calmed down, I moved close to Fimochka, took shelter at his side, and asked him quietly: "How do you feel, Fimochka?"

There was no answer. In the darkness I felt his arms and legs. He was not moving. There was no sign of life. I rose a bit and looked into his face. He was lying with closed eyes. I tried to open them until I realized that the boy was dead. Apparently the shot that was heard a moment earlier took his life.

I caressed the boy's cold face, bidding him farewell, then I stood up and started to run.

Only after making sure I was far away from that terrible place called Babi Yar did I allow myself to walk upright, to a hut that could barely be made out in the darkness … .

Source: Pronicheva, Dina and Yitzhak Arad (ed). "Testimony of Dina Pronicheva about the Annihilation of the Jews in Babi Yar," *The Destruction of the Jews of the USSR during the German Occupation*. Translated by Yad Vashem. Tel Aviv: Yad Vashem, 1991. Copyright © 1991 by Yad Vashem. Reprinted with permission.

READING 66

Stalin's Order #227 by the People's Commissar of the Defense of the USSR, Moscow, 1942

This became the standing order for all military actions from 1942 until the end of the war: no commander had the right to retreat without an order. The order also stipulated that each front must have at least one penal battalion made up of at least 800 middle-ranking commanders who had been identified as having disciplinary problems. Those penal battalions were sent to the most dangerous places on the front line. The order also created "blockade detachments" that would shoot or capture soldiers who fled from the front. Does this order seem reasonable? What justifications does Stalin use for the order? What might the implications of this order have been for soldiers on the ground?

The enemy feeds more and more resources to the front, and, paying no attention to losses, moves on, penetrates deeper into the Soviet Union, captures new areas, devastates and plunders our cities and villages, rapes, kills and robs the Soviet people. The fighting goes on in Voronezh, at the Don, in Southern Russia, at the gates of the North Caucasus. The German invaders are driving towards Stalingrad, towards the Volga, and want to capture Kuban and the North Caucasus with their oil and bread riches at any price. The enemy has already captured Voroshilovgrad, Starobelsk, Rossosh, Kupyansk, Valuiki, Novocherkassk, Rostov on Don, half of Voronezh. Some units of the south front, following the panic-mongers, have abandoned Rostov and Novocherkassk without serious resistance and without order from Moscow, thus covering their banners with shame.

The people of our country, who treat the Red Army with love and respect, are now starting to be disappointed with it, lose faith in the Red Army, and many of them curse the Army for its fleeing to the east and leaving the population under German yoke.

Some unwise people at the front comfort themselves with arguments that we can continue the retreat to the east, as we have vast territories, a lot of soil, many people, and that we will always have abundance of bread. By these arguments they try to justify their shameful behavior at the front. But all these arguments are fully false, faked and working for our enemies … .

READING 66 Stalin's Order #227 by the People's Commissar of the Defense of the USSR, Moscow, 1942

If we do not stop retreating, we will be left without bread, without fuel, without metals, without raw materials, without factories and plants, without railways.

The conclusion is that it is time to stop the retreat. Not a single step back! This should be our slogan from now.

We need to protect every strongpoint, every meter of Soviet soil stubbornly, till the last droplet of blood, grab every piece of our soil and defend it as long as it is possible. Our Motherland is going through hard times. We have to stop, and then throw back and destroy the enemy, whatever it might cost us. The Germans are not as strong as the panic-mongers say. They are stretching their strength to the limit. To withstand their blow now means to ensure victory in the future … .

From now on the iron law of discipline for every officer, soldier, political officer should be—not a single step back without order from higher command. Company, battalion, regiment and division commanders, as well as the commissars and political officers of corresponding ranks who retreat without order from above, are traitors of the Motherland. They should be treated as traitors of the Motherland. This is the call of our Motherland.

Source: McNeal, Robert H. ed. *Resolutions and Decisions of the Communist Party of the Soviet Union*. Vol. 3. Toronto: University of Toronto Press, 1974.

READING 67

Nazi Policies on the Eastern Front, 1943

While the previous reading brings home the hardness with which the Soviet regime managed its own troops, it is important to keep in mind what they were facing. In this piece, the Reichsfuehrer of the SS, Heinrich Himmler, spells out in detail the Nazi approach to the Eastern Front. How did the Nazi leadership talk about the populations of Eastern Europe? If you were a Soviet citizen, what would this speech mean to you and how you deal with the Nazis and the war?

One basic principal must be the absolute rule for the SS man: we must be honest, decent, loyal, and comradely to members of our own blood and to nobody else. What happens to a Russian, to a Czech, does not interest me in the slightest. What the nations can offer in good blood of our type, we will take, if necessary by kidnapping their children and raising them with us. Whether nations live in prosperity or starve to death interests me only in so far as we need them as slaves for our culture; otherwise, it is of no interest to me. Whether 10,000 Russian females fall down from exhaustion while digging an anti-tank ditch interests me only in so far as the anti-tank ditch for Germany is finished. We shall never be rough and heartless when it is not necessary, that is clear. We Germans, who are the only people in the world who have a decent attitude towards animals, will also assume a decent attitude towards these human animals. But it is a crime against our own blood to worry about them and give them ideals, thus causing our sons and grandsons to have a more difficult time with them. When someone comes to me and says, "I cannot dig the anti-tank ditch with women and children, it is inhuman, for it will kill them", then I would have to say, "you are a murderer of your own blood because if the anti-tank ditch is not dug, German soldiers will die, and they are the sons of German mothers. They are our own blood".

Source: Himmler, H. *Nazi Conspiracy and Aggression*. Vol. IV. Washington: U.S Govt. Print. Off., 1946.

READING 68

Diary of Valery Sukhov, A Child of Twelve, During the Leningrad Bombardment, 1941

The Siege of Leningrad began on September 8, 1941 and ended 872 days later on January 27, 1944. German Field Marshal Wilhelm Ritter von Leeb had orders to raze the city to the ground. His plan to capture the city was changed, however, when Hitler recalled the 4th Panzer Division to the Battle for Moscow. After that, the Germans and Finns adopted a siege policy, with a plan to starve the city of Leningrad into submission. And starve they did. An estimated 1.5 million people died due to starvation and bombardment. Economic destruction of the city was worse than the bombing of Tokyo. The Leningrad Bombardment is widely considered to be the most lethal siege in world history. And yet, despite the odds, the city never surrendered. In these next two pieces, figure out how much food Valery Sukhov would have had to eat in a day during the siege. Replicate that much food in your own kitchen.

23 December: Papa barely walks. Mama staggers. We're hoping for January [...] We cooked soup from carpenter's glue and ate all the starch [...] Papa is prepared to eat the corpses of those killed in the bombardment. Mama refuses. It's already been a whole month since we had solid food in our stomachs, besides the daily portion of bread of 125 grams, there's been nothing [...]

28 January: Papa died.

Source: State Memorial Museum of the Defense of and Blockade of Leningrad (GMMOBL), St. Petersburg, op. 1, d. 388. Cited in Bidlack, Richard and Nikita Lomagin eds. *The Leningrad Blockade*. New Haven: Yale University Press, 2012.

READING 69

Chart of Calorie Allotments for Leningrad Residents During the Siege, 1941

TABLE 1

FACTORY WORKERS AND ENGINEER-TECHNICAL WORKERS

Bread	250 grams
Fats	20 grams
Meat	50 grams
Cereals	50 grams
Sugar and Confectionery	50 grams
Total	420 grams (1,087 calories)

OFFICE WORKERS

Bread	125.0 grams
Fats	8.3 grams
Meat	26.6 grams
Sugar and Confectionery	33.3 grams
Cereals	33.3 grams
Total	226.5 grams (581 calories)

DEPENDENTS

Bread	125.0 grams
Fats	6.6 grams
Meat	13.2 grams
Sugar and Confectionery	26.6 grams
Cereals	20.0 grams
Total	191.4 grams (466 calories)

CHILDREN UNDER 12

Bread	125.0 grams
Fats	16.6 grams
Meat	13.2 grams
Sugar and Confectionery	40.0 grams
Cereals	40.0 grams
Total	234.8 grams (684 calories)

Source: Riha, Thomas. *Readings in Russian Civilization*. Vol. 3. Chicago: University of Chicago Press, 1969.

READING 70

Toast to the Russian People at a Reception in Honor of Red Army Commanders Given by the Soviet Government in the Kremlin on Thursday, May 25, 1945

No part of the Soviet Union was left untouched by the Great Patriotic War. At its end, 24 million people had died (compared to 400,000 in the United States), and the material damage was measured in the billions. In this speech, who is being thanked for the victory? What might the Soviet people have expected to happen after the war was over? Referring back to your textbook, how does this compare with what actually happened?

COMRADES! Permit me to propose one more, last toast.

I should like to propose a toast to the health of our Soviet people, and in the first place, the Russian people. (*Loud and prolonged applause and shouts of "Hurrah."*)

I drink in the first place to the health of the Russian people because it is the most outstanding nation of all the nations forming the Soviet Union.

I propose a toast to the health of the Russian people because it has won in this war universal recognition as the leading force of the Soviet Union among all the peoples of our country.

I propose a toast to the health of the Russian people not only because it is the leading people, but also because it possesses a clear mind, a staunch character, and patience.

Our Government made not a few errors, we experienced at moments a desperate situation in 1941–1942, when our Army was retreating, abandoning our own villages and towns of the Ukraine, Byelorussia, Moldavia, the Leningrad Region, the Baltic area and the Karelo-Finnish Republic, abandoning them because there was no other way out. A different people could have said to the Government: "You have failed to justify our expectations. Go away. We shall install another government which will conclude peace with Germany and assure us a quiet life." The Russian people, however, did not take this path because it trusted the correctness of the policy of its Government, and it made sacrifices to ensure the rout of Germany. This confidence of the Russian people in the Soviet Government proved to be that decisive force which ensured the historic victory over the enemy of humanity—over fascism.

Thanks to it, to the Russian people, for this confidence!

To the health of the Russian people! (*Loud and prolonged applause.*)

Source: "Speech at the Reception in the Kremlin in Honor of the Commanders of the Red Army Troops." *Pravda*, May 25, 1945.

READING 71

Stalin's "Two Camps" Speech, 1946

This is one of the many famous speeches that is now thought to have ushered in the Cold War. What is the topic of this speech? What caused the Great Patriotic War, according to Stalin? What does he argue has been proven by the Soviet victory? What policies of the 1930s does Stalin believe were justified by the War? What are the implications of these justifications in how we think about the events of the 1930s? If you were an American or British diplomat, how might you read this speech? What does all the applause say about Stalin's status at the end of the war?

Comrades!

Eight years have passed since the last elections to the Supreme Soviet. This has been a period replete with events of a decisive nature. The first four years were years of intense labor on the part of Soviet people in carrying out the Third Five-Year Plan. The second four years covered the events of the war against the German and Japanese aggressors—the events of the Great Patriotic War. Undoubtedly, the war was the main event during the past period.

It would be wrong to think that the Great Patriotic War broke out accidentally, or as a result of blunders committed by certain statesmen, although blunders were certainly committed. As a matter of fact, the war broke out as the inevitable result of the development of world economic and political forces on the basis of present-day monopolistic capitalism. Marxists have more than once stated that the capitalist system of world economy contains the elements of a general crisis and military conflicts, that, in view of that, the development of world capitalism in our times does not proceed smoothly and evenly, but through crises and catastrophic wars. The point is that the uneven development of capitalist countries usually leads, in the course of time, to a sharp disturbance of the equilibrium within the world system of capitalism, and that group of capitalist countries regards itself as being less securely provided with raw materials and markets usually attempts to change the situation and to redistribute "spheres of influence" in its own favor—by employing armed force. As a result of this, the capitalist world is split into two hostile camps, and war breaks out between them ... .

Thus, as a result of the first crisis of the capitalist system of world economy, the First World War broke out; and as a result of the second crisis, the Second World War broke out .... .

And so, how should our victory over the enemies be interpreted? What can this victory signify from the point of view of the state and the development of the internal forces of our country?

Our victory signifies, first of all, that our Soviet social system was victorious, that the Soviet social system successfully passed the test of fire in the war and proved that it is fully viable.

As we know, the foreign press on more than one occasion asserted that the Soviet social system was a "dangerous experiment" that was doomed to failure, that the Soviet system was a "house of cards" having no foundations in life and imposed upon the people by the Cheka, and that a slight shock from without was sufficient to cause this "house of cards" to collapse.

Now we can say that the war has refuted all these assertions of the foreign press and has proved them to have been groundless. The war proved that the Soviet social system is a genuinely people's system, which grew up from the ranks of the people and enjoys their powerful| support; that the Soviet social system is a fully viable and stable form of organization of society.

More than that, the issue now is not whether the Soviet social system is viable or not, because after the object lessons of the war, no skeptic now dares to express doubt concerning the viability of the Soviet social system. Now the issue is that the Soviet social system has proved to be more viable and stable than the non-Soviet social system, that the Soviet social system is a better form of organization of society than any non-Soviet social system.

Secondly, our victory signifies that our Soviet state system was victorious, that our multinational Soviet state passed all the tests of the war and proved its viability .... .

The issue now is no longer the viability of the Soviet state system, because there can be no doubt about its viability. Now the issue is that the Soviet state system has proved to be a model multinational state, that the Soviet state system is a system of state organization in which the national problem and the problem of the collaboration of nations have found a better solution than in any other multinational state.

Thirdly, our victory signifies that the Soviet Armed Forces, our Red Army, was victorious, that the Red Army heroically withstood all the hardships of the war, utterly routed the armies of our enemies, and emerged from the war the victor. (A voice: "Under Comrade Stalin's leadership!" All rise. Loud and prolonged applause, rising to an ovation.) .... .

The war proved that the Red Army is not "a colossus with feet of clay," but a first-class modern army, equipped with the most up-to-date armaments, led by most experienced commanders and possessing high morale and fighting qualities. It must not be forgotten that the Red Army is the army which utterly routed the German army, the army which only yesterday struck terror in the hearts of the armies of the European states.

By what policy was the Communist Party able to create these material potentialities in so short a time?

First of all by the Soviet policy of industrializing the country.

The Soviet method of industrializing the country differs radically from the capitalist method of industrialization. In capitalist countries, industrialization usually starts with light industry. In view of the fact that light industry requires less investments, that capital turnover is faster, and profits are made more easily than in heavy industry, light industry becomes the first object of industrialization, in those countries. Only after the passage of a long period of time, during which light industry accumulates profits and concentrates them in the banks, only after this, does the turn of heavy industry come and accumulation begin gradually to be transferred to heavy industry for the purpose of creating conditions for its expansion. But this is a long process, which takes a long time, running into several decades, during which you have to wait while the light industry develops and do without heavy industry. Naturally, the Communist Party, could not take this path. The Party knew that war was approaching, that it would be impossible to defend our country without heavy industry, that it was necessary to set to work to develop heavy industry as quickly as possible, and that to be belated in this matter meant courting defeat ... .

Secondly, by the policy of collectivizing agriculture.

To put an end to our backwardness in agriculture and to provide the country with the largest possible amount of market grain, cotton, and so forth, it was necessary to pass from small peasant farming to large-scale farming, for only large-scale farming can employ modern machinery, utilize all the achievements of agricultural science and provide the largest possible quantity of market produce. But there are two kinds of large-scale farming—capitalist and collective. The Communist Party could not take the capitalist path of developing agriculture not only on grounds of principle, but also because that path presupposes an exceedingly long process of development and requires the preliminary ruination of the peasants and their transformation into agricultural laborers. The Communist Party therefore took the path of collectivizing agriculture, the path of organizing large farms by uniting the peasant farms into collective farms. The collective method proved to be an exceedingly progressive method not only because it did not call for the ruination of the peasants, but also, and particularly, because it enabled us in the course of several years to cover the entire country with large collective farms capable of employing modern machinery, of utilizing all the achievements of agricultural science and of providing the country with the largest possible quantity of market produce.

...

Now a few words about the Communist Party's plans of work for the immediate future ... .As regards long-term plans, our Party intends to organize another powerful upswing of our national economy that will enable us to raise our industry to a level, say, three times as high as that of prewar industry. We must see to it that our industry shall be able to produce annually up to 50,000,000 tons of pig iron (prolonged applause), up to 60,000,000 tons of steel (prolonged applause), up to 500,000,000 tons of coal (prolonged applause) and up to 60,000,000 tons of oil (prolonged applause). Only when we succeed in doing that can we be sure that our Motherland will be insured against all contingencies. (Loud applause.) This will need, perhaps, another three five-year plans, if, not more. But it can be done, and we must do it. (Loud applause.)

...

In conclusion, permit me to express my thanks for the confidence which you have shown me (loud and prolonged applause. A voice: "Cheers for the great leader of all our victories, Comrade Stalin!") by nominating me as a candidate for the Supreme Soviet. You need have no doubt that I will do my best to justify your confidence. (All rise. Loud and prolonged applause rising to an ovation. Voices in different parts of the hall: "Long live great Stalin, Hurrah!" "Cheers for the great leader of the peoples!" "Glory to great Stalin!" "Long live Comrade Stalin, the candidate of the entire people!" "Glory to the creator of all our victories, Comrade Stalin!")

Source: Stalin, I.V. *Speeches Delivered at Meetings of Voters of the Stalin Electoral District, Moscow*. Moscow: Foreign Languages Publishing House, 1950.

READING 72

Stalin and the Cold War, 1946
Speech Delivered by Stalin at a Meeting of Voters of the Stalin Electoral District, Moscow

Stalin's lesser-known response to Churchill's "Iron Curtain" speech tells us much about the Soviet perspective on the European settlement after the Great Patriotic War. What justification does Stalin give for the Soviet Union's desire to support Communist-friendly governments in Eastern Europe? Given what you know about Russian and Soviet history, does this justification make some sense? What is Stalin's perspective on the popularity of Communist Parties in Europe? Go online and read Churchill's famous speech. How do these two speeches, in many ways, set the tone for the next forty years?

… In substance, Mr. Churchill now stands in the position of a firebrand of war. And Mr. Churchill is not alone here. He has friends not only in England but also in the United States of America … .

The Soviet Union has lost in men several times more than Britain and the United States together … . It may be that some quarters are trying to push into oblivion these sacrifices of the Soviet people which insured the liberation of Europe from the Hitlerite yoke.

But the Soviet Union cannot forget them. One can ask therefore, what can be surprising in the fact that the Soviet Union, in a desire to ensure its security for the future, tries to achieve that these countries should have governments whose relations to the Soviet Union are loyal? How can one, without having lost one's reason, qualify these peaceful aspirations of the Soviet Union as "expansionist tendencies" of our Government? …

Mr. Churchill wanders around the truth when he speaks of the growth of the influence of the Communist parties in Eastern Europe … . The growth of the influence of Communism cannot be considered accidental. It is a normal function. The influence of the Communists grew because during the hard years of the mastery of fascism in Europe, Communists showed themselves to be reliable, daring, and self-sacrificing fighters against fascist regimes for the liberty of peoples.

Source: Stalin, I.V. "Stalin's Reply to Churchill," (interview with Pravda). *The New York Times,* March 14, 1946.

chapter NINE

From De-Stalinization to the Brezhnev Doctrine, 1953–1968

READING 73

Vladimir Pomerantsev, "On Sincerity in Literature," 1953

Vladimir Pomerantsev published this piece not long after Stalin's death. With it, he changed the direction of Soviet art and started the process of encouraging writers, painters, and filmmakers to think more critically about the problems of Socialist Realism. Look at when Pomerantsev wrote this essay. What is so critical about this date (and why could he not have written it one year earlier)? What is Pomerantsev implicitly attacking here? What is his critique of Soviet literature? What does this piece tell us about the changes happening in the Soviet Union in these years, and what is its significance for the future?

Insincerity—this is not necessarily a lie. Artificiality is also insincere.

When we read, for example, the stylists, we are left with an unpleasant aftertaste. We see too many carefully sought-out, chosen, and mannered thoughts and words; we strain too much to follow the manner of the writing, and, therefore, we miss its substance. These works are complicated, artificially complex, and they oppress today's reader with their obvious construction.

But there I was reading a novel which had no stylistics—for it had no style in general—and it left me just as cold as those books filled with coquettish tricks. I have in mind *The Deciding Years* by S. Boldyrev. The artificiality in this work arises not from the manner of writing, but from the far-fetched nature of the characters and the situations. This, so to speak, is another mode of the construction of novels and tales.

The boredom arising from S. Bodyrev's book might be explained by his literary helplessness. But its basic vice lies in its obvious construction. Of course, a struggle was waged and continues to be waged at the nation's metallurgic factories for the optimal use of blast furnaces. But this struggle can become a fact of literature only if the thoughts and feelings of the writer are included in it. But there is none of that in *Deciding Years*. Seemingly, everything in this book is correct; but from the point of view of art, everything is absolutely wrong. We don't feel the soul of the author here, we don't get to know his own thoughts. All we get is something too well known, having no emotional basis, and flavored with the cult of the personality of the novel's hero. Therefore, one cannot believe in the characters in this book. The hero here is a superhero. He is planned out, premeditated, made up, perpetrated. In the novel, certainly, there are no sins against the technology of metallurgy or against the organization of blast furnace production. But it contains an unpardonable sin against art: it is an artificial novel.

Source: Pomerantsev, Vladimir. "On Sincerity in Literature," Translated by Seventeen Moments in Soviet History. *Novyi Mir*. Dec, 1953.

READING 74

Cartoon of Khrushchev, the "Kukuruznik," 1956

One of the key components of Khrushchev's Virgin Lands program was the plan to cultivate corn in the Soviet Union. He considered himself an expert on agriculture and was convinced that the growing of corn would allow for the increase in fodder for livestock. Looking at this image, how did satirists criticize Khrushchev's plan for corn cultivation? Can you decipher the many little meanings that are planted in this drawing? What does it say about Soviet culture that the satirical newspaper, *Krokodil*, could publish such a depiction of the General Secretary?

Source: "Kukuruza." *Krokodil*. June 10, 1956.

READING 75

The Warsaw Security Pact, 1955

The Soviet Union and its satellite powers in Eastern Europe entered into the Warsaw Pact in 1955. After reading this declaration, can you guess what precipitated its signing? What did they all agree to on the surface, and what did they all agree to in reality? What justifications did they provide for joining? What were the implications of the Warsaw Pact's creation, and how would this become a critically important organization in 1956 and in 1968?

Treaty of Friendship, Cooperation and Mutual Assistance Between the People's Republic of Albania, the People's Republic of Bulgaria, the Hungarian People's Republic, the German Democratic Republic, the Polish People's Republic, the Rumanian People's Republic, the Union of Soviet Socialist Republics and the Czechoslovak Republic, May 14, 1955.

The Contracting Parties, reaffirming their desire for the establishment of a system of European collective security based on the participation of all European states irrespective of their social and political systems, which would make it possible to unite their efforts in safeguarding the peace of Europe; mindful, at the same time, of the situation created in Europe by the ratification of the Paris agreements, which envisage the formation of a new military alignment in the shape of "Western European Union," with the participation of a remilitarized Western Germany and the integration of the latter in the North-Atlantic bloc, which increased the danger of another war and constitutes a threat to the national security of the peaceable states; ... have agreed as follows:

ARTICLE 1

The Contracting Parties undertake, in accordance with the Charter of the United Nations Organization, to refrain in their international relations from the threat or use of force, and to settle their international disputes peacefully and in such manner as will not jeopardize international peace and security.

ARTICLE 2

The Contracting Parties declare their readiness to participate in a spirit of sincere cooperation in all international actions designed to safeguard international peace and security, and will fully devote their energies to the attainment of this end.

The Contracting Parties will furthermore strive for the adoption, in agreement with other states which may desire to cooperate in this, of effective measures for universal reduction of armaments and prohibition of atomic, hydrogen and other weapons of mass destruction.

ARTICLE 3

The Contracting Parties shall consult with one another on all important international issues affecting their common interests, guided by the desire to strengthen international peace and security.

They shall immediately consult with one another whenever, in the opinion of any one of them, a threat of armed attack on one or more of the Parties to the Treaty has arisen, in order to ensure joint defense and the maintenance of peace and security.

ARTICLE 4

In the event of armed attack in Europe on one or more of the Parties to the Treaty by any state or group of states, each of the Parties to the Treaty, in the exercise of its right to individual or collective self-defense in accordance with Article 51 of the Charter of the United Nations Organization, shall immediately, either individually or in agreement with other Parties to the Treaty, come to the assistance of the state or states attacked with all such means as it deems necessary, including armed force. The Parties to the Treaty shall immediately consult concerning the necessary measures to be taken by them jointly in order to restore and maintain international peace and security.

Measures taken on the basis of this Article shall be reported to the Security Council in conformity with the provisions of the Charter of the United Nations Organization. These measures shall be discontinued immediately the Security Council adopts the necessary measures to restore and maintain international peace and security.

Source: U.S. Department of State. *American Foreign Policy, 1950–1955, Basic Documents*. Volume 1. Department of State Publication 6446. General Foreign Policy Series 117. Washington, DC: Government Printing Office, 1957.

READING 76

Khrushchev's "Destalinization" Speech, 1956

The Twentieth Party Congress was a watershed in the political history of modern Russia. It was the first since Stalin's death. The Congress started in a humdrum fashion. Then, on the evening of February 25, 1956, the delegates were summoned to an unscheduled speech given by Khrushchev. The speech took four hours for Khrushchev to deliver. In the years that followed, dissident populations across the Soviet Union heard the speech and took it as a sign that change was coming. The speech was a spark for the 1956 Hungarian Revolution. It launched an outpouring of innovative art, literature, and film known as "The Thaw" that tentatively questioned some of the foundations of Socialist Realism. In this short excerpt, can you see why this speech was so revolutionary? How did Khrushchev attack Stalin? What criticisms did Khrushchev levy at the now-dead leader and what criticisms did he NOT levy? Can you speculate on the consequences that this speech would have on the Soviet Union and Eastern Europe?

During Lenin's life the central committee of the party was a real expression of collective leadership of the party and of the Nation. Being a militant Marxist-revolutionist, always unyielding in matters of principle, Lenin never imposed by force his views upon his coworkers. He tried to convince; he patiently explained his opinions to others. Lenin always diligently observed that the norms of party life were realized, that the party statute was enforced, and that the party congresses and the plenary sessions of the central committee took place at the proper intervals.

In addition to the great accomplishments of V. I. Lenin for the victory of the working class and of the working peasants, for the victory of our party and for the application of the ideas of scientific communism to life, his acute mind detected in Stalin those negative characteristics which resulted later in grave consequences. Fearing the future fate of the party and of the Soviet nation, V. I. Lenin made a completely correct characterization of Stalin, pointing out that it was necessary to consider the question of transferring Stalin from the position of Secretary General because of the fact that Stalin is excessively rude, that he does not have a proper attitude toward his comrades, that he is capricious, and abuses his power … .

As later events have proven, Lenin's anxiety was justified ... .

Stalin acted not through persuasion, explanation, and patient cooperation with people, but by imposing his concepts and demanding absolute submission to his opinion. Whoever opposed this concept or tried to prove his viewpoint and the correctness of his position was doomed to removal from the leading collective and to subsequent moral and physical annihilation. This was especially true during the period following the 17th party congress, when many prominent party leaders and rank-and-file party workers, honest and dedicated to the cause of communism, fell victim to Stalin's despotism ... .

Stalin originated the concept of "enemy of the people."... This concept, "enemy of the people," actually eliminated the possibility of any kind of ideological fight or the making of one's views known on this or that issue, even those of a practical character. In the main, and in actuality, the only proof of guilt used, against all norms of current legal science, was the confession of the accused himself, and, as subsequent probing proved, confessions were acquired through physical pressures against the accused ... .

Lenin used severe methods only in the most necessary cases, when the exploiting classes were still in existence and were vigorously opposing the revolution, when the struggle for survival was decidedly assuming the sharpest forms, even including a civil war.

Stalin, on the other hand, used extreme methods and mass repressions at a time when the revolution was already victorious, when the Soviet state was strengthened, when the exploiting classes were already liquidated, and Socialist relations were rooted solidly in all phases of national economy, when our party was politically consolidated and had strengthened itself both numerically and ideologically. It is clear that here Stalin showed in a whole series of cases his intolerance, his brutality, and his abuse of power. Instead of proving his political correctness and mobilizing the masses, he often chose the path of repression and physical annihilation, not only against actual enemies, but also against individuals who had not committed any crimes against the party and the Soviet Government. Here we see no wisdom but only a demonstration of the brutal force which had once so alarmed V. I. Lenin ... .

Stalin's willfulness vis-a-vis the party and its central committee became fully evident after the 17th party congress, which took place in 1934 ... .

It was determined that of the 139 members and candidates of the party's Central Committee who were elected at the 17th congress, 98 persons, that is, 70 percent, were arrested and shot (mostly in 1937–38). [Indignation in the hall.] ... .

The same fate met not only the central committee members but also the majority of the delegates to the 17th party congress. Of 1,966 delegates with either voting or advisory rights, 1,108 persons were arrested on charges of anti-revolutionary crimes, i.e., decidedly more than a majority. This very fact shows how absurd, wild, and contrary to commonsense were the charges of counter-revolutionary crimes made out, as we now see, against a majority of participants at the 17th party congress. [Indignation in the hall.] ... .

After the criminal murder of S. M. Kirov, mass repressions and brutal acts of violation of Socialist legality began.

The mass repressions at this time were made under the slogan of a fight against the Trotskyites. Did the Trotskyites at this time actually constitute such a danger to our party and to the Soviet state? We should recall that in 1927, on the eve of the 15th party congress, only some 4,000 votes were cast for the Trotskyite-Zinovievite opposition, while there were 724,000 for the party line ... .

Now when the cases of some of these so-called spies and saboteurs were examined it was found that all their cases were fabricated. Confessions of guilt of many who were arrested and charged with enemy activity were gained with the help of cruel and inhuman tortures ... .

An example of vile provocation of odious falsification and of criminal violation of revolutionary legality is the case of the former candidate for the central committee political bureau, one of the most eminent workers of the party and of the Soviet Government, Comrade Eikhe, who was a party member since 1905. [Commotion in the hall.]

Comrade Eikhe was arrested on April 29, 1938, on the basis of slanderous materials, without the sanction of the prosecutor of the USSR, which was finally received 15 months after the arrest.

Investigation of Eikhe's case was made in a manner which most brutally violated Soviet legality and was accompanied by willfulness and falsification.

Eikhe was forced under torture to sign ahead of time a protocol of his confession prepared by the investigative judges, in which he and several other eminent party workers were accused of anti-Soviet activity.

On February 2, 1940, Eikhe was brought before the court. Here he did not confess any guilt and said as follows:

"In all the so-called confessions of mine there is not one letter written by me with the exception of my signatures under the protocols which were forced from me. I have made my confession under pressure from the investigative judge who from the time of my arrest tormented me. After that I began to write all this nonsense. The most important thing for me is to tell the court, the party and Stalin that I am not guilty. I have never been guilty of any conspiracy. I will die believing in the truth of party policy as I have believed in it during my whole life."

On February 4 Eikhe was shot. [Indignation in the hall.] It has been definitely established now that Eikhe's case was fabricated; he has been posthumously rehabilitated ... .

Source: U.S. Congress. *Congressional Record: Proceedings and Debates of the 84th Congress, 2nd Session.* C11, Part 7, June 4, 1956.

READING 77

Pravda Announces the Soviet Invasion of Hungary, 1956

The clearest response to Khrushchev's Secret Speech could be seen in Eastern Europe where subject populations took the speech to be a sign that Soviet control was loosening. In the summer and fall of 1956, the people of Hungary took steps to break away from the Warsaw Pact and to endorse a new, progressive leader, Imre Nagy. The Soviet response was to crush the rebellion, sending in troops on the same day that this article was published in the State newspaper, *Pravda*. The Hungarian resistance fought the Soviet invaders until November 10. An estimated 2,500 Hungarians and 700 Soviet troops were killed in the uprising, and arrests continued for months afterward. For the thirty years that followed, discussion of the uprising was expressly forbidden. In this piece, *Pravda*, announces the decision to intervene in Hungary. How does *Pravda* "pitch" this story? Who is to blame for what is happening, and what is the Soviet Union's role in "helping" the Hungarian people?

"The events in Hungary have attracted the attention of the whole world. The Soviet people, who feel great friendship and brotherliness towards the people of Hungary, have been stirred by the successes and difficulties faced by the Hungarian workers in the struggle for the development of their country on the path to socialism.

A million Soviet people warmly sympathize with the efforts of the Hungarian workers to help their people successfully develop a free and sovereign socialist government ... .

At the same time, one cannot fail to see ... the actions of the reactionary forces, which are deeply alien to the people, which are clearly evident in the events of the last days in Hungary. They are aimed at destroying the socialist gains of the working people and restoring capitalism in the country. These anti-people elements, who are harkening to the mistakes of the past, and are resorting to demagogic slogans and hiding behind the false mask of "fighters for freedom," are trying to deceive and entice the masses of the working people. One cannot, of course, mistake honestly erring young people with those counter-revolutionary elements that treacherously deceive them. These elements are hostile to the people, they do not work for the interests of the working people, they hate socialism."

Source: "To Block the Reactionary Path in Hungary!" (Peregradit' Put' Reaktsii v Vengrii!). Translated by the Margaret Peacock. *Pravda*. November 4, 1956.

READING 78

Yuri Gagarin's Parade after Returning from Space, 1961

Yuri Gagarin was the first human in space. He completed an orbit of the earth in his Vostok space craft on April 12, 1961. This was a momentous event in world history, not just because it was man's first leap into space, but because it was a critical Soviet victory in the ongoing Space Race. By 1961, the Soviets were well ahead of the United States in the race to space. In 1956, they had launched the satellite, Sputnik, and in 1957 had sent the dog Laika in orbit around the earth. As you read this announcement of Gagarin's triumph, think about how the Soviet press portrays him and his accomplishment. What kind of message were Gagarin's voyage and his exultant reception back home supposed to convey to the rest of the world? Why did the Space Race matter so much in these years?

On April 14, the Soviet people welcomed their fearless and courageous son, Hero of the Soviet Union, the first space pilot of our planet, Major Yuri Alexeyevich Gagarin.

The whole city rejoiced. The roads and squares were decorated with flags, bright panels and streamers. Portraits of the 27-year-old pilot were held aloft. Everywhere there were flags, banners and flowers. There were queues at the booths selling postcards with portraits of the first cosmonaut.

By mid-day, thousands of people with happy faces filled the streets. Strains of the melodies of favorite songs flowed from the loudspeakers, songs about the homeland, the Party and its heroes which glorified the world's first socialist power.

The Soviet people celebrated the great event as a national holiday.

The 33-kilometer road between Vnukovo airport, where the cosmonaut arrived, and Red Square, the center of our capital, seemed to have become the main thoroughfare of our planet. The Columbus of space was to arrive here by plane from the area where the spaceship Vostok landed. Although one could get into Vnukovo only by special pass, thousands of Muscovites waited there for the hero for a long time. Along the road, in an endless stream, cars and buses were decorated with colorful flags and garlands. Nearly everybody carried bouquets of flowers.

Gathered at the airfield were representatives of working people, Soviet and foreign public figures, scientists and diplomats. And every one of them, like the people all over the world, was moved by the unexampled flight of the Soviet cosmonaut.

N.S. Khrushchev arrived at Vnukovo from Sochi by special plane at 12:30 to meet the hero.

...

Moscow's Red Square! Many notable pages in the history of our country are bound up with it. Every year military parades, demonstrations of working people and sports parades are arranged there.

The 22-meter space rocket erected in Red Square symbolizes a new era into which man has entered, an era of the conquest of space opened by the genius of the Soviet people.

Source: Soviet Press Reports. *The First Man in Space: The Record of Yuri Gagarin's Historic First Venture into Cosmic Space, A Collection of Translations from Soviet Press Reports.* New York: Crosscurrents Press Inc., 1961.

READING 79

Evgenii Yevtushenko, "Stalin's Heirs," 1962

In 1962, writers, artists, and filmmakers started to really test the boundaries of the State's tolerance for dissident work. Two writers, Evgenii Yevtushenko and Viktor Nekrasov, wrote powerful attacks on the Soviet regime. This poem hit readers like a bomb. It was written and copied and shared from person-to-person and was the topic of conversation across kitchen tables among friends who trusted each other. What is Yevtushenko really attacking in this poem? Is he really afraid that Stalin will come back from the dead, or is there some other, far more likely, form of reincarnation that scares him? Who does Yevtushenko blame for the Great Terror and, in your opinion, is there anything missing in that critique?

The marble was silent.
The glass glistened silently.
The guards stood silent,
Bronzing in the sun.
But the coffin gave off a faint vapor.
Breath leaked through a crack
When they took it through the Mausoleum doors.
The coffin slowly floated past,
Its corners touching the bayonets.
He too was silent too! –
But frighteningly silent.
Sullenly clenching
Embalmed fists,
Inside, the man pretending death
Pressed against the crack.
He wanted to remember all those
Who were carrying him out:

Young Ryazan and Kursk recruits, So that
    afterward somehow
He might gather the strength for a sally
And rise from the earth
And get at these rash persons.
He had thought of something.
He had merely nestled down for a rest.
And I appeal to our government
With the request
To double,
To triple
The guard at this slab
So that Stalin may not rise,
And, with Stalin,
The past.
I am not speaking of that treasured, valorous past
    which was Turksib,

Magnitka
And the flag over Berlin.
Here
I mean by the past
The ignoring of the people's welfare,
The calumnies,
The arrests of the innocent.
We sowed honestly.
We poured steel honestly
And we marched honestly,
Lining up in soldiers' ranks.
But he feared us.
Believing in a great goal, he did not believe
That the means
Should be worthy of the great goal.

Source: Evtushenko, Evgenii. "Stalin's Heirs," *Current Digest of the Soviet Press*, vol. 14, no. 40. Copyright © 1963 by East View Information Services, Inc. Reprinted with permission.

READING 80

Prime Minister Fidel Castro's Letter to Chairman Khrushchev, 1962

The Cuban Missile Crisis brought the world to the brink of nuclear war. American intelligence had known for some time that the Soviets were installing nuclear launch pads on Cuban soil. When an American U2 spy plane confirmed the existence of medium- and intermediate-range missile facilities in Cuba, President John F. Kennedy's government ordered a blockade of Cuban waters. This would prevent the Soviets from making any further shipments to Cuba. Over thirteen days in the fall of 1962, no one could be sure whether or not Khrushchev would turn back the Soviet ships headed to Cuba or push through the blockade and potentially start World War III. In the end, Kennedy and Khrushchev came to an agreement, and the Soviet ships turned around. In the middle of all this, Khrushchev also had to deal with Fidel Castro, the Communist leader of Cuba, who had very different feelings about what Khrushchev should do. Read Castro's letter to Khrushchev, written in the middle of the crisis. What decision does he want Khrushchev to make? What justifications does he give for his opinions? What kind of relationship do you think Khrushchev and Castro had?

Havana, October 26, 1962

Dear Comrade Khrushchev:

From an analysis of the situation and the reports in our possession, I consider that the aggression is almost imminent within the next 24 or 72 hours.

There are two possible variants: the first and likeliest one is an air attack against certain targets with the limited objective of destroying them; the second, less probable although possible, is invasion. I understand that this variant would call for a large number of forces and it is, in addition, the most repulsive form of aggression, which might inhibit them.

You can rest assured that we will firmly and resolutely resist attack, whatever it may be.

The morale of the Cuban people is extremely high and the aggressor will be confronted heroically.

At this time I want to convey to you briefly my personal opinion.

If the second variant is implemented and the imperialists invade Cuba with the goal of occupying it, the danger that that aggressive policy poses for humanity is so great that following that event the Soviet Union must never allow the circumstances in which the imperialists could launch the first nuclear strike against it.

I tell you this because I believe that the imperialists' aggressiveness is extremely dangerous and if they actually carry out the brutal act of invading Cuba in violation of international law and morality, that would be the moment to eliminate such danger forever through an act of clear legitimate defense, however harsh and terrible the solution would be, for there is no other.

It has influenced my opinion to see how this aggressive policy is developing, how the imperialists, disregarding world public opinion and ignoring principles and the law, are blockading the seas, violating our airspace and preparing an invasion, while at the same time frustrating every possibility for talks, even though they are aware of the seriousness of the problem.

You have been and continue to be a tireless defender of peace and I realize how bitter these hours must be, when the outcome of your superhuman efforts is so seriously threatened. However, up to the last moment we will maintain the hope that peace will be safeguarded and we are willing to contribute to this as much as we can. But at the same time, we are ready to calmly confront a situation which we view as quite real and quite close.

Once more I convey to you the infinite gratitude and recognition of our people to the Soviet people who have been so generous and fraternal with us, as well as our profound gratitude and admiration for you, and wish you success in the huge task and serious responsibilities ahead of you.

Fraternally,

Fidel Castro

Source: Castro, Fidel. *Personal Letters*. The National Security Archive at The George Washington University, The Cuban Missile Crisis, 1962: The Documents. Reprinted with permission.

READING 81

Letter from Khrushchev to Castro, 1962

Here is Khrushchev's letter back to Castro. Summarize Khrushchev's response. Do you think Castro would be happy with this answer? What justifications does Khrushchev give for his decision?

Dear Comrade Fidel Castro:

Our October 27 message to President Kennedy allows for the question to be settled in your favor, to defend Cuba from an invasion and prevent war from breaking out. Kennedy's reply, which you apparently also know, offers assurances that the United States will not invade Cuba with its own forces, nor will it permit its allies to carry out an invasion. In this way the president of the United States has positively answered my messages of October 26 and 27, 1962.

We have now finished drafting our reply to the president's message. I am not going to convey it here, for you surely know the text, which is now being broadcast over the radio. With this motive I would like to recommend to you now, at this moment of change in the crisis, not to be carried away by sentiment and to show firmness. I must say that I understand your feelings of indignation toward the aggressive actions and violations of elementary norms of international law on the part of the United States. But now, rather than law, what prevails is the senselessness of the militarists at the Pentagon. Now that an agreement is within sight, the Pentagon is searching for a pretext to frustrate this agreement. This is why it is organizing the provocative flights. Yesterday you shot down one of these, while earlier you didn't shoot them down when they overflew your territory. The aggressors will take advantage of such a step for their own purposes. Therefore, I would like to advise you in a friendly manner to show patience, firmness and even more firmness. Naturally, if there's an invasion it will be necessary to repulse it by every means. But we mustn't allow ourselves to be carried away by provocations, because the Pentagon's unbridled militarists, now that the solution to the conflict is in sight and apparently in your favor, creating a guarantee against the invasion of Cuba, are trying to frustrate the agreement and provoke you into actions that could be used against you. I ask you not to give them the pretext for doing that. On our part, we will do everything possible to stabilize the situation in Cuba, defend Cuba against invasion, and assure you of the possibilities for peacefully building a socialist society. I send you greetings, extensive to all your leadership group.

N. Khrushchev
October 28, 1962

Source: Khrushchev, Nikita. *Personal Letters*. The National Security Archive at The George Washington University, The Cuban Missile Crisis, 1962: The Documents. Reprinted with permission.

READING 82

The Soviet Invasion of Czechoslovakia, 1968
The Warsaw Letter

Brezhnev and the Warsaw Pact members sent this letter to the new, reform-minded Communist president of Czechoslovakia, Alexander Dubček, in the summer of 1968. Earlier that year, Dubček's government had embraced a policy of "Socialism with a human face" that included liberalizations in politics and public expression. These months would come to be known as the Prague Spring. By the end of the summer, Brezhnev and the other Conservative leaders of the Warsaw Pact were becoming increasingly worried that the Communist Party of Czechoslovakia was losing control. In the wake of this letter, Dubček and Brezhnev agreed to bilateral talks. This did not stop the process of liberalization, however, and on August 20, 1968, Eastern Bloc armies from four Warsaw Pact countries invaded Czechoslovakia. As in Hungary, they put down the uprising with brutal force. Does this letter bear any resemblance to the *Pravda* article on Hungary in 1956? If so, how? Can you pick out recurring phrases and arguments? Do some additional reading to see if the outcome of the Czechoslovak invasion was the same as in Hungary. If there were differences, what were they and how can you explain them?

The development of events in your country evokes deep anxiety in us. It is our deep conviction that the offensive of the reactionary forces, backed by imperialism, against your party and the foundations of the socialist system in the Czechoslovak Socialist Republic threatens to push your country off the road of socialism and thus jeopardizes the interests of the entire socialist system ... We cannot agree to have hostile forces push your country from the road of socialism and create a threat of severing Czechoslovakia from the socialist community. This is something more than your cause. It is the common cause of our countries, which have joined in the Warsaw Pact ... .

You are aware of the understanding with which the fraternal parties treated the decisions of the January plenary meeting of the Central Committee of the Communist Party of Czechoslovakia, as they believed that your party, firmly controlling the levers of power, would direct the entire process in the interest of socialism and not let anti-Communist reaction exploit it to grind its own ax. We shared the conviction that you would protect and cherish the Leninist principle of democratic centralism ... .

Unfortunately, events have taken another course.

Capitalizing on the weakening of party leadership in the country and demagogically abusing the slogan of "democratization," the forces of reaction triggered off a campaign against the Communist Party of Czechoslovakia and its honest and devoted cadres, clearly seeking to abolish the party's leading role, subvert the socialist system, and place Czechoslovakia in opposition to the other socialist countries ... .

Anti-socialist and revisionist forces have laid hands on the press, radio and television, making them a rostrum for attacking the Communist Party, disorienting the working class and all working folk, spewing forth uncurbed anti-socialist demagogy, and undermining friendly relations between the Czechoslovak Socialist Republic and the other socialist countries ... .

Czechoslovakia can retain her independence and sovereignty only as a socialist country, as a member of the socialist community ... It is our conviction that a situation has arisen in which the threat to the foundations of socialism in Czechoslovakia jeopardizes the common vital interests of other socialist countries ... .

That is why we believe that a decisive rebuff to the forces of anti-communism and decisive efforts to preserve the socialist system in Czechoslovakia are not only your task but ours, too.

The cause of defending the power of the working class and of all working people, as well as Czechoslovakia's socialist gains, demands that a bold and decisive offensive should be launched against right-wing and anti-socialist forces; that all the defensive means set up by the socialist state should be mobilized; that a stop should be put to the activity of all political organizations that come out against socialism; that the party should take control of the mass-information media—press, radio, and television—and use them in the interests of the working class, of all working people, and of socialism; that the ranks of the party itself should be closed on the principled basis of Marxism-Leninism; that the principle of democratic centralism should be undeviatingly observed; and that a struggle should be undertaken against those whose activity helps the enemy ... .

We express the conviction that the Communist Party of Czechoslovakia, conscious of its responsibility, will take the necessary steps to block the path of reaction. In this struggle, you can count on the solidarity and all-around assistance of the fraternal socialist countries.

Source: Lowenthal, Richard. "The Sparrow in the Cage," *Problems of Communism*, 17, no. 6 (Nov-Dec 1968): 2–28.

READING 83

The Brezhnev Doctrine, 1968

The Brezhnev Doctrine was announced in September 1968 to retroactively justify the Soviet invasion of Czechoslovakia. It carried the message that only limited sovereignty would be granted to the satellite states of the Soviet Union and that the period of liberalization was officially over. What justifications do you see for this doctrine here? Can you unpack this convoluted language to see what is really being arguing here?

In connection with the events in Czechoslovakia the question of the correlation and interdependence of the national interests of the socialist countries and their international duties acquire particular topical and acute importance. The measures taken by the Soviet Union, jointly with other socialist countries, in defending the socialist gains of the Czechoslovak people are of great significance for strengthening the socialist community, which is the main achievement of the international working class. We cannot ignore the assertions, held in some places that the actions of the five socialist countries run counter to the Marxist Leninist principle of sovereignty and the rights of nations to self-determination. The groundlessness of such reasoning consists primarily in that it is based on an abstract, non-class approach to the question of sovereignty and the rights of nations to self-determination. The peoples of the socialist countries and Communist parties certainly do have and should have freedom for determining the ways of advance of their respective countries. However, none of their decisions should damage either socialism in their country or the fundamental interests of other socialist countries, and the whole working class movement, which is working for socialism. This means that each Communist party is responsible not only to its own people, but also to all the socialist countries, to the entire Communist movement. ... .

The socialist countries resolutely come out against the exporting and importing of counterrevolution. Each Communist party is free to apply the basic principles of Marxism Leninism and of socialism in its country, but it cannot depart from these principles (assuming, naturally, that it remains a Communist party). Concretely, this means, first of all, that, in its activity, each Communist party cannot but take into account such a decisive fact of our time as the struggle between two opposing social systems-capitalism and socialism … .

The weakening of any of the links in the world system of socialism directly affects all the socialist countries, which cannot look indifferently upon this. The antisocialist elements in Czechoslovakia actually covered up the demand for so-called neutrality and Czechoslovakia's withdrawal from the socialist community with talking about the right of nations to self-determination. However, the implementation of such "self-determination," in other words, Czechoslovakia's detachment from the socialist community, would have come into conflict with its own vital interests and would have been detrimental to the other socialist states. Such "self-determination," as a result of which NATO troops would have been able to come up to the Soviet border, while the community of European socialist countries would have been split, in effect encroaches upon the vital interests of the peoples of these countries and conflicts, as the very root of it, with the right of these people to socialist self-determination.

Source: Brezhnev, L. "The Brezhnev Doctrine." *Pravda,* September 25, 1968, cited in Stavrianos, L.S. *The Epic of Man*. Translated by Novosti. Englewood Cliffs, N.J.: Prentice-Hall, 1971.

chapter TEN

Soviet Stagnation and Collapse, 1968–1991

READING 84

Economic Stagnation, 1960–1985
Chart of the Slowing of the Soviet Economy

Net Material Product (NMP) was the primary macroeconomic indicator for tracking economic growth in Socialist countries during the Soviet period. It roughly resembles the Gross National Product of the West (as you can see in this chart). It measures material production in industry, agriculture, transportation, construction, but not the service sector. What can you derive from this chart? Can you explain the differences between the GNP and the NMP and how those numbers change from 1960 to 1985? What is the significance of these numbers for understanding the Soviet Union in the 1970s and 80s?

PERIOD	GROWTH RATES (IN BILLIONS OF RUBLES)		
	GNP (ACCORDING TO THE CIA)	NMP (ACCORDING TO G. I. KHANIN)	NMP (ACCORDING TO THE USSR)
1960–1965	4.8	4.4	6.5
1965–1970	4.9	4.1	7.7
1970–1975	3.0	3.2	5.7
1975–1980	1.9	1.0	4.2
1980–1985	1.8	0.6	3.5

Source: Bacon, Edwin and Mark Sandle. *Brezhnev Reconsidered*. New York: Palgrave MacMillan, 2000.

READING 85

The Problem of Supply and Demand, 1971
A. Levashova, "Fashion and Economics"

The Brezhnev period is frequently characterized by one word: stagnation. While elite members of the Soviet nomenclatura enjoyed nice apartments and travel abroad, the majority of citizens learned to accept lives that were marked by shortages. At least the hulking leviathan of the Soviet state guaranteed employment, a pension, and freedom from the random terror of the 1930s. Ironically, because of this normalization, the Soviet populace increasingly demanded a better standard of living. There were those who saw that the centralized state was failing to meet the growing expectations of the population. What is the critique of centralized planning laid out in this excerpt? What is the significance is of this piece and what are the implications of Levashova being able to publish this?

Trade organizations should have good information about the demands and tastes of the public. It must be admitted, however, that trade outlets and industry alike have as yet studied demand insufficiently and do not always respond quickly to the changes in it. We do not have shops specializing in selling the latest fashions.

Instead of carefully getting ready in advance to update the line of goods, instead of studying demand, industry waits for the trade outlets to place their orders. More and more often now one can see women wearing long skirts in the theater and long coats on the street. These are still generally homemade articles. Garment makers could manufacture them of higher quality and better design. Yet, the trade outlets intend only in 1972 to order about 20% of women's clothing in maxi lengths.

Autumn and spring coats in the styles made by factories during the past two years are already beginning to pile up in stores and warehouses.

The problems stemming from fashion become increasingly acute as the broad market becomes more saturated with goods. The main barrier here is psychological. Should we make fitted or loose trousers, long or short skirts and coats? These are questions that no one undertakes to decide until the woman in the street sets the style.

The trouble is that we have practically no rational system of production and introduction of stylish goods. The functioning of the design organizations, the manufacturers and the trade outlets is not coordinated. A group of clothing items that should make up an ensemble is turned out in a mixture of styles; after buying a coat, you will spend a lot of time before you can find the right bag, hat or shoes. The fashion councils of the various enterprises are not in touch with one another, and it turns out that, for example, the lining fabrics turned out by the Moscow silk combines generally do not match the color of the woolens that the Moscow Liberated Labor and Petr Alekseev mills produce for coats. The colors of fabrics are changed less often than they should be. Very often "forgotten" fabrics, such as, for example, gabardine at the moment, cashmere, crepe, and certain others, become fashionable.

...

One of the factors hindering the issue of new articles is the complicated procedure for approval of designs, technical specifications and prices. This procedure takes many months. The price lists currently in effect make it unprofitable to manufacture whole categories of women's clothing which are either completely missing from the garment makers' product mix (lined suits, velveteen pants) or are turned out in insufficient numbers (women's silk blouses). When the prices for the new articles are set, often they do not meet even the average profitability of other, analogous articles.

What conclusion suggests itself from the above? We must have a precise system for developing and introducing styles, under which, on the basis of thorough study of demand, it would be possible to organize mass production of new styles in a short time. Effective methods of forecasting are necessary, methods which can answer the questions not only of how much and where clothing, footwear and other goods will be demanded today and tomorrow, but also in what exact mixes, colors and average price.

The introduction of style innovations could be organized expediently in the following manner. The All Union Institute of Planning the Assortment of Goods of Light Industry and Fashion, together with the industry institutes, would prepare recommendations with respect to fabrics and decorative materials, on the basis of the real economic potential of the industry. Experimental lots of the new fabrics would be turned out in sufficient numbers to guarantee small-series production.

The fashion design houses would work up collections of new designs and issue them in trial series at experimental production facilities. The articles would go into stores specializing in the latest fashions. There the demand for small lots of imported goods could also be tested before purchasing in quantity. Advertising of the new articles would be organized simultaneously. The stores, together with the fashion design houses, would sum up and analyze the demand data. The trade organizations would use these data for making up sound mass orders from industry. After this, the fashion houses would turn over to the enterprises the specifications for the popular models, tested in experimental production to meet all technological requirements, and the enterprises would proceed to mass produce the goods. ...

Source: A Levashova, "Fashion and Economics," *Current Digest of the Soviet Press*, vol. 23, no. 19. Copyright © 1971 by East View Information Services, Inc. Reprinted with permission.

READING 86

The War in Afghanistan, 1979

The Soviet government drafted this directive in December of 1979, authorizing the introduction of Soviet troops into Afghanistan. Before you read this, review your textbook or the Internet to learn what events had transpired in the previous two years. When you return here, read this directive and ask yourself what justifications for intervention are being given? How is the situation in Afghanistan being painted? Given what we know about the outcome of the Soviet-Afghan war, what mistakes did the Soviet leadership make right from the onset?

"Considering the military-political situation in the Middle East, the latest appeal of the government of Afghanistan has been favorably considered. The decision has been made to introduce several contingents of Soviet troops deployed in southern regions of the country to the territory of the Democratic Republic of Afghanistan in order to give international aid to the friendly Afghan people and also to create favorable conditions to interdict possible anti-Afghan actions from neighboring countries … ."

Source: Lyakhovskiy, A.A. "Plamya Afgana." Translated by Gary Goldberg. Moscow: Iskon, 1999.

READING 87

The Decree Against Alcohol, 1985

In 1985, as a part of his reforms, Gorbachev launched a massive, anti-alcohol campaign. The state raised the price of alcohol significantly, and although it was initially successful in cutting back the amount of alcohol purchased, it had the unintended consequence of spawning the production of dangerous moonshine (called "*samogen*" in Russian) and decreasing the critical revenue that had previously come from the taxing of alcohol. By 1994, in the wake of the Soviet Union's collapse, life expectancy rates reached an all-time low. What does this decree say about the Soviet Union in the mid-1980s? What population of people do you think the second paragraph is targeting?

The drinking of spirits during production (in the place of work, in buildings and on the premises of enterprises, institutions and organizations) or being drunk at work is liable to an administrative penalty, in the form of a fine to the sum of 30 to 50 roubles … .

The purchase and resale for the sale of gain of small amounts of vodka and other liquors, as well as mass consumption goods and agricultural products, till and sale receipts and bills, entertainment and other tickets, books, music notes, records, audio and video cassettes and other valuables, if the scale of profit does not exceed 30 roubles, is liable to an administrative penalty in the form of a fine of 50–100 roubles with the confiscation of the items being speculated.

Source: Spravochnik partiinogo rabotnika, vypusk 26. Moscow: Partizdat, 1986, 617–623. Cited in Sakwa, Richard ed. *The Rise and Fall of the Soviet Union, 1917–1991.* London: Routledge, 1999.

READING 88

The Chernobyl Disaster, 1986

On April 25–26, 1986, the Chernobyl nuclear power plant in northern Ukraine experienced a catastrophic meltdown. A combination of design and maintenance errors led to a massive steam explosion and open fire which released as much as 5.6 roentgens per second into the surrounding area. Emergency workers received lethal radioactive doses in less than a minute. In order to avoid a public relations nightmare, the Soviet government chose not to evacuate the nearby city of Pripyat. On April 26, this report from the first deputy minister of Energy and Electrification made its way to the Central Committee in Moscow. Read the report now, keeping in mind that on April 27, the next day, a gradual evacuation began. In the following days, the Soviet Government chose not to tell the world about what had happened and downplayed the scale of the disaster. It went ahead with a massive outdoor parade on May 1 in Kiev despite the dangerous radiation levels. Some historians now number the long term casualties of the Chernobyl disaster between 30,000 and 40,000. What socio-political structures had to be in place for this report below to have been written? Why were authorities so scared to tell the truth? What do you think the consequences of this were for upholding the legitimacy of the Soviet Union?

APRIL 26, 1986
URGENT REPORT

On April 26, 1986, at 1:21 A.M., in taking Chernobyl AES generating unit No. 4 off-load for planned repairs, after shutting down the reactor, an explosion took place in the upper part of the reactor compartment.

According to the report of the Chernobyl AES directory, in the explosion of the roof, part of the wall panels of the reactor compartment, several roof panels of the generator room, and the reactor compartment's auxiliary systems block collapsed, and also the roofing caught fire.

At 3:30 A.M. the fire was extinguished.

Through the efforts of the AES personnel, measures are being taken to cool down the reactor core.

In the opinion of Main Administration 3 of the USSR Ministry of Heath, implementation of special measures, including evacuation of the city's population, is not necessary.

Nine operations staff members and 25 paramilitary fire fighters were hospitalized.

Measures are being taken to remove the aftereffects and to investigate the incident.

Source: Koenker, Diane and Ronald Bachman. *Revelations from the Russian Archives.* Washington DC: Library of Congress, 1997.

READING 89

Perestroika, 1988
Letter from Georgy Shakhnazarov to Mikhail Gorbachev

Georgy Sakhnazarov was one of Gorbachev's top aids. Read this critique of the economic problems in the Socialist bloc and ask yourself, "Could any official have been able to write anything like this in the 1950s?" Focusing on the third paragraph here, what point is Shakhnazarov making and what are the implications of this?

Today we are discussing the results of our talks with the leaders or prominent figures from a number of socialist countries … .

Each country has its unique situation and we would be correct not to approach them across-the-board [*chokhom*]; we are seeking to figure out the specifics of each of them, and to build our policy on the basis of such an analysis … .

Notwithstanding all their differences and nuances, there are multiple signs that some similar problems are increasingly plaguing the fraternal countries. The very similarity of symptoms of the disease testifies to the fact that its catalyst [*vozbuditel*] is not some kind of a malignant germ that has managed to penetrate their lowered defenses, but some factors rooted in the very economic and political model of socialism as it had evolved over here, and has been transferred with insignificant modifications to the soil of the countries who had embarked on the path of socialism in the postwar period.

We have already laid bare weaknesses of this model and are beginning to remove them in a systematic way. This is actually the super-task of perestroika—to give socialism a new quality … .

When we receive from time to time alarmist cables we do what we can, but all this is at best like applying lotion to sores, not a systematic, thoughtful strategy for treatment of the disease, not to mention preventive measures. It is high time to discuss these issues at the Politburo in the presence of experts. We should not bury our head in the sand like an ostrich, but we should look into the future with open eyes and ask ourselves the sharpest questions … .

This is a huge problem, in scope as well as in significance, we need to tackle it continuously, but the first exchange should take place as early as late December [1988]-early January 1989. There will be a working conference of the Party leadership of the commonwealth in Prague in February, and this gives us a chance to share some of our conclusions with our friends.

Source: Shakhnazarov, Georgy. *Letter form Georgey Shakhnazarov to Mikhail Gorbachev.* October 6, 1988. Translated by Vladislav Zubok. Cold War International History Project Archive, Documents and Papers, 1988. Reprinted with Permission

READING 90

Gorbachev Speaks to the UN, 1988
Excerpts of Address by Mikhail Gorbachev to the 43rd UN General Assembly

Mikhail Gorbachev gave this monumental speech to the UN General Assembly at the end of 1988. Read through it, and write down all the points that Gorbachev is making. What message does he clearly have for the countries that make up the Soviet Bloc? What message does he have for the United States? Why do you think Gorbachev made the decision to follow these new policies? Was it simply a desire to be fair, or was he aware of larger global and economic factors that necessitated these new policies? What were those factors?

Two great revolutions, the French revolution of 1789 and the Russian revolution of 1917, have exerted a powerful influence on the actual nature of the historical process and radically changed the course of world events. Both of them, each in its own way, have given a gigantic impetus to man's progress. They are also the ones that have formed in many respects the way of thinking which is still prevailing in the public consciousness.

That is a very great spiritual wealth, but there emerges before us today a different world, for which it is necessary to seek different roads toward the future, to seek—relying, of course, on accumulated experience—but also seeing the radical differences between that which was yesterday and that which is taking place today.

The newness of the tasks, and at the same time their difficulty, are not limited to this. Today we have entered an era when progress will be based on the interests of all mankind. Consciousness of this requires that world policy, too, should be determined by the priority of the values of all mankind.

The history of the past centuries and millennia has been a history of almost ubiquitous wars, and sometimes desperate battles, leading to mutual destruction. They occurred in the clash of social and political interests and national hostility, be it from ideological or religious incompatibility. All that was the case, and even now many still claim that this past—which has not been overcome—is an immutable pattern. However, parallel with the process of wars, hostility, and alienation of peoples and countries, another process, just as objectively conditioned, was in motion and gaining force: The process of the emergence of a mutually connected and integral world.

Further world progress is now possible only through the search for a consensus of all mankind, in movement toward a new world order. We have arrived at a frontier at which controlled spontaneity leads to a dead end. The world community must learn to shape and direct the process in such a way as to preserve civilization, to make it safe for all and more pleasant for normal life. It is a question of cooperation that could be more accurately called "co-creation" and "co-development." The formula of development "at another's expense" is becoming outdated. In light of present realities, genuine progress by infringing upon the rights and liberties of man and peoples, or at the expense of nature, is impossible.

The very tackling of global problems requires a new "volume" and "quality" of cooperation by states and sociopolitical currents regardless of ideological and other differences … .

It is evident, for example, that force and the threat of force can no longer be, and should not be instruments of foreign policy … .

The compelling necessity of the principle of freedom of choice is also clear to us. The failure to recognize this, to recognize it, is fraught with very dire consequences, consequences for world peace. Denying that right to the peoples, no matter what the pretext, no matter what the words are used to conceal it, means infringing upon even the unstable balance that is, has been possible to achieve … .

Our country is undergoing a truly revolutionary upsurge. The process of restructuring is gaining pace; we started by elaborating the theoretical concepts of restructuring; we had to assess the nature and scope of the problems, to interpret the lessons of the past, and to express this in the form of political conclusions and programs. This was done … .

In order to involve society in implementing the plans for restructuring it had to be made more truly democratic. Under the badge of democratization, restructuring has now encompassed politics, the economy, spiritual life, and ideology. We have unfolded a radical economic reform, we have accumulated experience, and from the new year, we are transferring the entire national economy to new forms and work methods. Moreover, this means a profound reorganization of production relations and the realization of the immense potential of socialist property.

Now about the most important topic, without which no problem of the coming century can be resolved: disarmament … .

Today I can inform you of the following: The Soviet Union has made a decision on reducing its armed forces. In the next two years, their numerical strength will be reduced by 500,000 persons, and the volume of conventional arms will also be cut considerably. These reductions will be made on a unilateral basis, unconnected with negotiations on the mandate for the Vienna meeting … .

Finally, being on U.S. soil, but also for other, understandable reasons, I cannot but turn to the subject of our relations with this great country … .

Relations between the Soviet Union and the United States of America span 5 1/2 decades. The world has changed, and so have the nature, role, and place of these relations in world politics. For too long they were built under the banner of confrontation, and sometimes of hostility, either open or concealed. But in the last few years, throughout the world people were able to heave a sigh of relief, thanks to the changes for the better in the substance and atmosphere of the relations between Moscow and Washington.

No one intends to underestimate the serious nature of the disagreements, and the difficulties of the problems which have not been settled. However, we have already graduated from the primary school of instruction in mutual understanding and in searching for solutions in our and in the common interests. The U.S.S.R. and the United States created the biggest nuclear missile arsenals, but after objectively recognizing their responsibility, they were able to be the first to conclude an agreement on the reduction and physical destruction of a proportion of these weapons, which threatened both themselves and everyone else … .

The future U.S. administration headed by newly elected President George Bush will find in us a partner, ready—without long pauses and backward movements—to continue the dialogue in a spirit of realism, openness, and goodwill, and with a striving for concrete results, over an agenda encompassing the key issues of Soviet-U.S. relations and international politics.

Source: Gorbachev, Mikhail. "Address by Mikhail Gorbachev at the UN General Assembly Session (Excerpts)." 43rd U.N. General Assembly Session, December 7, 1988. History and Public Policy Program Digital Archive, Cold War International History Project Archive. Reprinted with permission.

READING 91

"Assessing the Future of the Soviet Military," 1989

Read this entry and the next to get a sense of the state of the Soviet Union and its precarious hold on power in the late 1980s. Who wrote this excerpt? What is the significance of these people coming to these conclusions about the state of the Soviet military? What transformation in the global balance of power does this seem to be signaling?

SOVIET CUTBACKS

In December 1988, Gorbachev announced at the United Nations that significant unilateral reductions of Soviet forces would take place in 1989 and 1990. His statement was followed by various explanations of Soviet reduction plans and additional announcements concerning cuts in defense spending and production. Soon after Gorbachev's announcement, each of the USSR's Warsaw Pact Allies except Romania announced force and defense spending cuts. These cuts—to be completed by the end of 1990—roughly parallel the Soviet cuts in types and proportional amounts of equipment, manpower, and expenditures.

EFFECTS OF THE CHANGES

Reductions and restructuring will significantly degrade the ability of Soviet forces to concentrate combat power, particularly for offensive operations. Armored striking power, in particular, is reduced and fragmented. The new motorized rifle divisions are well suited for defensive operations but are not organized specifically to conduct large-scale attacks or counterattacks. The new tank divisions are "balanced"—thus, better suited for holding ground than the previous standard tank divisions—but they retain substantial offensive punch.

COMBAT POTENTIAL

To gauge the probability of mission success, Soviet staff officers often compare the relative strength of opposing forces in terms of their calculated "combat potential." How the Soviets come up with combat [section blacked out] it is useful to essay a Soviet-style combat-potential analysis to see how the Soviets might view the correlation of forces in Europe following their unilateral reductions and restructuring.

Source: National Intelligence Council. "Assessing the Future of the Soviet Military," Making the History of 1989 Archive, George Madison University, Item #190.

READING 92

The Soviet Economy, 1990

In 1987, the General Secretary of the Soviet Union, Mikhail Gorbachev, introduced the reform idea of Perestroika. It would be a thorough renewal of the entire Soviet social system, with an end goal of stopping the country's economic decline. Unfortunately, as the program unfolded, Gorbachev realized that Perestroika was dying in the swamp of the Soviet bureaucracy. Even the smallest reforms were failing because the system itself had lost its ability to change. And so, Gorbachev introduced a second reform idea, Glasnost, which would allow the people to talk openly about their problems and, hopefully, jump-start the needed reforms. In 1989, the famed American political cartoonist Jim Borgman published this illustration in the *Cincinnati Enquirer* as a commentary on the state of Soviet reforms. In the cartoon, a mechanic stands amidst the pieces of a disassembled car with the words, "Perestroika Motors" printed on his overalls. Above him hovers the shell of the car, labeled "Soviet Economy." What is Borgman saying here about the state of the Soviet Union? What, in his opinion, has the Soviet Union succeeded in doing? Is Borgman saying something about whether or not Perestroika was worth attempting at all? This illustration represents a remarkably ambiguous perspective on Perestroika for its time. Across the United States, journalists and politicians lauded Gorbachev for his reforms, and yet, in some ways, is Borgman not arguing here that the Soviet Union would have been better off not attempting to reform?

Source: The Opper Project

READING 93

The Map of the Commonwealth of Independent States, 1991

In 1991, the Soviet Union collapsed and the map of Eastern Europe and the Caucasus changed drastically. Spend some time studying this map. Many of these countries underwent revolutions of their own as they struggled to transition to a capitalist economy and to a representative government. Some were more successful than others.

Source: Central Intelligence Agency. "Commonwealth of Independent States, Map 1994," Making the History of 1989 Archive, George Madison University, Item #393.

READING 94

Boris Yeltsin's "Tank" Speech, August 19, 1991

In August 1991, hardline Communists in the Soviet government attempted a coup against Gorbachev while he was on vacation on the Crimean coast. However, they failed to arrest the President of the Congress of People's Deputies, Boris Yelstin, who quickly rallied supporters and headed to the White House to defend Gorbachev's government. The military chose to side with Yeltsin. He famously climbed atop a tank that was guarding the White House to deliver this speech. The coup failed, and Gorbachev quickly moved to return to Moscow. When he returned, he found that his power had faded under Yeltsin's rising preeminence. Read this excerpt from Yeltsin's famous "Tank" speech. What argument does he make? Is there a line here that resonates for you and if so, why?

Citizens of Russia: On the night of 18–19 August 1991, the legally elected president of the country was removed from power.

Regardless of the reasons given for his removal, we are dealing with a rightist, reactionary, anti-constitutional coup. Despite all the difficulties and severe trials being experienced by the people, the democratic process in the country is acquiring an increasingly broad sweep and an irreversible character.

The peoples of Russia are becoming masters of their destiny ....

We appeal to citizens of Russia to give a fitting rebuff to the putschists and demand a return of the country to normal constitutional development.

Undoubtedly it is essential to give the country's president, Gorbachev, an opportunity to address the people. Today he has been blockaded. I have been denied communications with him. We demand an immediate convocation of an extraordinary Congress of People's Deputies of the Union. We are absolutely confident that our countrymen will not permit the sanctioning of the tyranny and lawlessness of the putschists, who have lost all shame and conscience. We address an appeal to servicemen to manifest lofty civic duty and not take part in the reactionary coup.

Until these demands are met, we appeal for a universal unlimited strike.

Source: Yeltsin, Boris. "Yeltsin's Remarks: A Reactionary Coup." *New York Times*, August 20, 1991.

READING 95

"Yeltsin Disbands Parliament, Calls Elections to 'Federal Assembly'," 1993

In the fall of 1993, a standoff happened between Yeltsin, the President, and the elected conservative Russian Parliament. This event has come to be called the "Constitutional Crisis" of 1993. Their relationship had been deteriorating for the last two years, as the Parliament repeatedly attempted to slow down the pace of reform (through legal means). Yeltsin responded by giving this speech over Russian television. Read through the speech, and see if you can tell what he is really doing here. The new Russian Constitution closely resembled the United States Constitution in the separation of differing branches of government. Whether you agree with Yeltsin or not, did he have the power to do what he did?

Esteemed fellow citizens, I am speaking to you at one of the most complicated and weighty moments, on the eve of extremely important events.

In recent months, Russia has been going through a deep crisis of statehood. Literally, all state institutions and politicians have been drawn into a fruitless and senseless fight to the death.

The direct consequence of this has been the lowering of the authority of state power as a whole. I am sure that all citizens of Russia have seen for themselves that in such conditions it is impossible not only to bring in very difficult reforms, but even to maintain elementary order.

It must be said straight out that if an end is not put to political confrontation by the authorities in Russia, if their work is not restored to their normal rhythm, the situation cannot be kept under control, our state cannot be preserved, and peace in Russia cannot be preserved.

Demands are flooding in to me from all corners of our country: halt the dangerous development of events; stop people's power from being mocked.

For over a year now attempts have been made to find a compromise with the corps of deputies, with the Supreme Soviet. The people of Russia know very well how many steps toward compromise have been made on my part at the most recent congresses, and in the periods between them. But even if it proved possible to reach agreement on something, in a short time there would follow a categorical refusal to fulfill the obligation undertaken ... .

The majority of the Supreme Soviet is embarking on the direct flouting of the will of the Russian people. A course is being pursued aimed at the weakening and eventual removal of the president, and at the disorganization of the work of the present government. A powerful propaganda campaign has been unleashed, aimed at the total discrediting of all executive power in Russia … .

The Supreme Soviet has stopped taking into account any of the president's decrees, his amendments to legislative acts, and even his constitutional right to veto. At the same time, it never ceases swearing its loyalty to the Constitution and the law. Constitutional reform has practically been discontinued … .

The laws that Russia needs so badly are not being adopted for years. Instead, radical revision of the existing Constitution and the already adopted legislative acts has begun. They get rewritten to suit political moods of the time. A shameful practice of judicial arbitrariness has gained a foothold here, and its essence is best expressed in a primitive formula: Whatever law we wish to adopt, we will adopt, we will write them as we see fit … .

Open and ostentatious vote cheating has become a daily occurrence: Those who take part in the sessions vote for those who are absent, several absentees' voting cards being used at one time, and this for the whole world to see … .

It is my duty as president to acknowledge that the present legislative corps has forfeited the right to be at the major levers of state power. The security of Russia and its peoples is of higher value than formal compliance with the contradictory norms created by a legislative power that has finally discredited itself. The time has come for the most serious decisions.

Esteemed compatriots, the only way of overcoming the paralysis of state power in the Russian Federation is its radical renovation on the basis of the principles of people's power and constitutionality. The existing Constitution does not allow this. Nor does the existing Constitution envisage a procedure of adopting a new Constitution providing for a dignified exit from the crisis of statehood.

Being the guarantor of the security of our state, I am obliged to propose a way out of this deadlock, I am obliged to break this ruinous vicious circle.

Taking into account the numerous appeals to me by the leaders of subjects of the Russian Federation, deputies' groups, participants in the Constitutional Conference, political parties, representatives of the public, and Russian citizens, I have undertaken the following: being vested with authority in the 1992 nationwide elections—and Russian citizens confirmed their confidence in this authority at the April 1993 referendum—I have approved, by my decree, amendments and addenda to the current Constitution of the Russian Federation. They bear mainly upon the federal bodies of legislative and executive authority, and their mutual relations on the basis of the principle of division of authorities … .

In keeping with the President's decree, which has already been signed, as of today, the implementation of the legislative, executive and supervisory functions of the Congress of People's Deputies and the Supreme Soviet of the Russian Federation ceases. Meetings of the Congress will no longer by convened. The powers of the people's deputies of the Russian Federation cease. Their labor rights, of course, will be guaranteed in full. The deputies have the right to return to the enterprises and institutions where they worked prior to being elected as Russia's deputies, and to occupy their previous posts. At the same time, each of them have the right to resubmit their candidacies for election to the Federal Assembly … .

Esteemed fellow citizens, the time has come when by joining forces together, we can and must put an end to the deep crisis of the Russian statehood. I count on your understanding and support. I count on your common sense and sense of civic duty. We do have a chance to help Russia … . Let us preserve Russia for ourselves and our children.

Source: Yeltsin, Boris. "Yeltsin Disbands Parliament, Calls Elections to 'Federal Assembly'." Moscow Ostankino Television First Channel Network. Foreign Broadcast Information Service (FBIS), 9-21-1993.

chapter ELEVEN
Post-Soviet Russia

READING 96

"Russia's Economic Transition," 2013

Can you use your text and these readings to explain the graph below? What year did Vladimir Putin come into power, and do you think this graph can help you to explain his popularity?

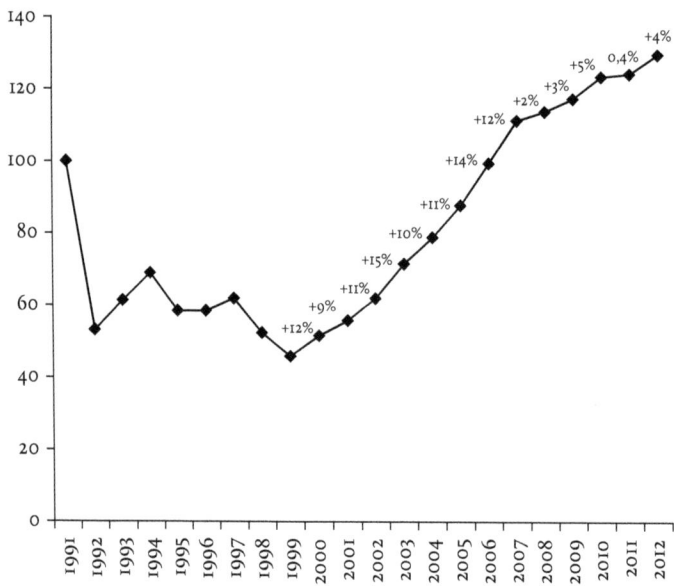

Source: Aven, Denis. "Russia's Economic Transition." *Yale Economic Review,* April 3, 2013.

READING 97

Russian Per Capita GDP and Global GDP Growth Rate Since the Fall of the Soviet Union, 1990–2015

What are the factors that can explain this graph? Given that the red line represents global growth and the blue line represents Russia, where can you see significant discrepancies? Can you explain the causes of them? What might be the significance of the graph for how we think about Russia today?

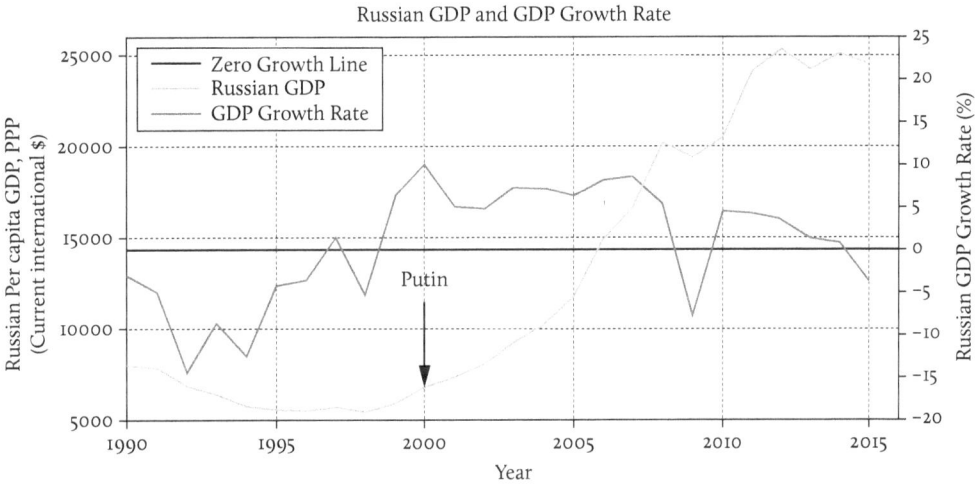

Source: Statistics compiled by Margaret Peacock from data provided by the Worldbank.

READING 98

Male Life Expectancy in Russia and the United States, 2000

This graph has much to say about what it was like to live in Russia in the last forty years of the twentieth century. Can you use male life expectancy rates as a gauge for understanding much larger social and economic transformations? Does this chart help to understand how domestic policy can have a concrete effect on the way people live their lives?

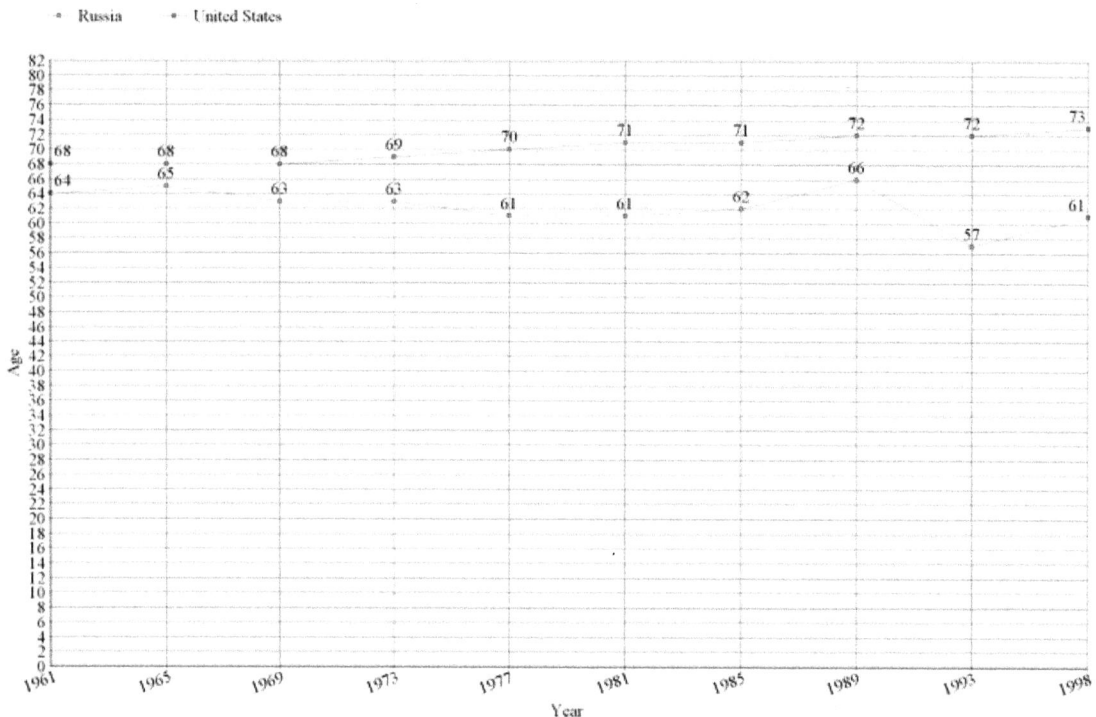

Source: Haaga, John. "High Death Rate Among Russian Men Predates Soviet Union's Demise." *The Population Reference Bureau,* April, 2000.

READING 99

Russian Parliament Suspends Yeltsin and Swears in Rutskoy, 1993

Here we see a news report on how the Russian Parliament responded to Yeltsin's order to dissolve the country's legislature. This did not end the crisis. Thousands took to the streets in support of the Parliament members, eventually seizing the mayor's office and the national television center. Nonetheless, the army chose to side with Yeltsin. It stormed the White House where the Parliament members had been residing. It arrested the Parliamentary leaders and restored Yeltsin to power. These ten days produced the deadliest street fighting in Moscow since the Revolution, with an estimate 200-2000 deaths. That December, Yeltsin managed to push through a new constitution that gave the president strong executive powers. Was this a legal action? Given that Yeltsin represented a force for reform while the Parliament was interested in retaining more of the old systems, can you make a decision about whether or not Yeltsin made the "right" decision in storming the White House? What happens when legality and morality come into conflict?

MOSCOW ITAR-TASS WORLD SERVICE IN RUSSIAN 2110 GMT 21 SEP 93

[By IT AR-TASS Parliamentary correspondent Ivan Novikov)

[Text] Moscow, 22 Sep—On the evening of 21 September, the Russian Supreme Soviet adopted a resolution to suspend the powers of President Boris Yeltsin. This decision was adopted by the majority of the deputies at midnight.

The resolution states that it was adopted "in connection with the Russian president's gross violation of the Constitution by issuing a decree on 21 September 1993 'On stage-by-stage constitutional reform in the Russian Federation,' which suspends the activity of legally elected bodies of state power."

Another resolution was also adopted, according to which Vice President Aleksandr Rutskoy will become acting president of the Russian Federation. He has already taken the oath.

However, the current Constitution does not stipulate that the president can by removed from power simply by a vote in parliament.

Source: TASS World Service. "Russian Parliament Suspends Yeltsin, Swears in Rutskoy." September 21, 1993. Foreign Broadcast Information Service (FBIS) 9-21-1993.

READING 100

"Troops Enter Chechnya to 'Restore Order,'" 1994

Chechnya has a long and tumultuous history with Russia. The country became a part of the Russian empire in the late nineteenth century after forty years of resistance. In 1944, an estimated half-million Chechens were ethnically cleansed and deported to Siberia under accusations of loyalty to the Germans. After the collapse of the Soviet Union, Chechnya was the only ethnic enclave to refuse to sign a treaty that would have made it a federated part of Russia. Relations worsened as Chechnya's once-popular leader, Dzhokar Dudayev, made moves to consolidate power and dissolve the Chechen Parliament. While many Chechens were dissatisfied with Dudayev (and raised arms against him), all Chechens agreed that independence from Russia was critical. This did not sit well with Yeltsin's government, which ordered the invasion of Chechnya on December 11, 1994. Read this radio transcript of the invasion announcement. What justifications does the Russian press give for the invasion? How is the invasion portrayed? In the year to come, Russian forces swept across Chechnya, destroying much of the capital city of Grozny, with an estimated 27,000 Chechen civilians dead in the first five weeks of fighting and 35,000 killed in the bombardment of Grozny. Chechan forces resorted to mass hostage-taking, the use of child soldiers, and the planting of improvised explosive devices. Peace was finally declared at the end of 1996. The war had been deeply unpopular in Russia, with the world community (along with dissidents inside Russia) speaking out against Russian human rights abuses.

TROOPS ENTER CHECHNYA TO 'RESTORE ORDER'

12074094 Moscow ITAR-TASS World Service in Russian 0705GMT11 Dec 94

[FBIS Translated Text] Moscow, 11 Dec (IT ART ASS)—implementing the decree of the Russian Federation president on the disarming of illegal armed formations and the restoration of constitutional order, this morning armed groups of Russian Federation Defense Ministry and Russian Federation interior Ministry troops, moving in three columns, entered the territory of the Chechen Republic. An ITAR-TASS correspondent learned this from the press service of the Russian Federation Government today.

The columns are advancing at a speed of up to 20 km an hour in the direction of the city of Groznyy. No clashes have been recorded. The population of the regions through which the columns are advancing is remaining calm.

As a preliminary, the report of the press service of the Government of the Russian Federation says, conditions for the evacuation of the civilian population, in the first place children, women and old people, have been secured. This will enable the part of the edict of the president of the Russian Federation which speaks of disarming all groups operating illegally on the territory of the Chechen Republic to be implemented ... .

The Government of the Russian Federation is taking every measure to maintain constitutional order on the territory of the Chechen Republic and protect the population reliably from any manifestation of violence whatsoever on the part of extremist groups and formations. Rear subunits of the Ministry of Defense and the interior troops of the Russian Federation are taking measures to supply the population with everything necessary, including food, the report of the press service of the Government of the Russian Federation says.

Source: TASS World Service. "Troops Enter Chechnya to 'Restore Order.'" December 11, 1994. Foreign Broadcast Information Service (FBIS) 11-12-1994.

READING 101

Yeltsin's "Resignation" Speech, 1999

Boris Yeltsin unexpectedly resigned at the end of 1999. By then, he had been largely delegitimized in the eyes of the world and his fellow Russians. He was accused of nepotism, of public drunkenness, of prolonging the Chechen War, and of allowing a small group of powerful ex-Communists-turned-Capitalists (commonly referred to as "The Oligarchs") to exploit and derail the country. Russian society was in dire straits, with a rising mortality rate, plummeting birth rates, and crises in housing, employment, and infrastructure. Read Yeltsin's resignation. What reasons for his resignation does he give? Do you think there might be other explanations for this decision?

Boris Yeltsin: Dear Russians,

In a few hours we will see a magical date on our calendars, the year 2000, a new century, a new millennium.

All of you tried to figure out, first as children and then as young people, how old you would be in the year 2000, and how old your mum and then your children would be. We thought that unique New Year was still very far in the future. But here it is.

Dear friends, my dear friends.

Today I am sending you my last New Year's greetings. But that's not all: this is the last time I am addressing you as president of Russia.

I have taken a decision, one which I pondered long and painfully. I am resigning today, the last day of the departing century.

I have heard people say more than once that Yeltsin would cling to power as long as possible, that he would never let go. That is a lie. I have always said that I would never violate the Constitution, that the parliamentary elections must be held in the timeframe stipulated by the Constitution, and this is exactly how we acted. I also wanted the presidential election to be held as planned, in June 2000. This is very important for Russia. We are creating a vital precedent of a civilized and voluntary transfer of presidential power to a newly elected president. And yet, I have taken a different decision: I am leaving before the end of my term.

I saw that I had to do this. Russia should enter the new millennium with new politicians, new faces, new people who are intelligent, strong and energetic, while we, those who have been in power for many years, must leave.

When I saw the hope with which the people voted for a new generation of politicians in the parliamentary elections, I knew that my life's work was done. Russia will never retrace its steps; it will keep moving into the future. And I must not stand in the way of that logical progression. Why cling to power for six more months when the country has a strong leader who can be its president, a man on whom nearly all Russians are pinning their hopes for the future? Why stand in his way? Why wait another half year? That is not for me.

Today, on this extremely important day for me, I want to say a few more personal words than I usually do. I want to ask your forgiveness—for the dreams that have not come true, and for the things that seemed easy but turned out to be so excruciatingly difficult. I am asking your forgiveness for failing to justify the hopes of those who believed me when I said that we would leap from the grey, stagnating totalitarian past into a bright, prosperous and civilized future. I believed in that dream, I believed that we would cover the distance in one leap.

We didn't. I was too naive in some things, and the problems turned out to be bigger than expected in other things. We ploughed ahead through mistakes and failures. Many people were traumatized by that time of upheavals.

I want you to know—I have never said this before, and I want to say it now—that the pain of every one of you was my pain, the pain of my heart. I spent sleepless nights, agonized thinking about what could be done to make life easier, if only a bit, for the people. It was my highest goal.

I am leaving now. I have done everything I could. I am not leaving for health reasons, but for a multitude of reasons. A new generation is taking my place, a generation of people who can do more and better.

In accordance with the Constitution, I have signed a decree giving the powers of president of Russia to Prime Minister Vladimir Putin. He will be the head of state for three months, after which presidential elections will be held, also in accordance with the Constitution.

I have always believed in the tremendous wisdom of the Russian people, and therefore I have no doubt about the choice you will make in late March 2000.

We are parting now, and I want to wish happiness to every one of you. You deserve it; you deserve happiness and peace of mind.

Happy New Year! Happy New Millennium!

Source: Yeltsin, Boris. "Statement by Boris Yeltsin, President of Russia." December 31, 1999. Kremlin Presidential Transcripts. Copyright © (CC by 4.0) at http://en.kremlin.ru/events/president/transcripts/24080.

READING 102

Election Results: 2000, 2004, 2008

These are the national election results for the President of the Russian Federation from 2000 to 2008. Look closely at the names, party affiliations, the numbers of votes, and the percentages of votes received. What conclusions can you draw about the changing nature of the political landscape in Russia through these years? Go and look at the most recent election. How has this office changed since 2008?

2000

CANDIDATE	PARTY	VOTES	%
Vladimir Putin	Independent	39,740,467	53.4
Gennady Zyuganov	Communist Party	21,928,468	29.5
Grigory Yavlinsky	Yabloko	4,351,450	5.9
Aman Tuleyev	Independent	2,217,364	3.0
Vladimir Zhirinovsky	Liberal Democratic Party	2,026,509	2.7
Konstantin Titov	Independent	1,107,269	1.5
Ella Pamfilova	For Civic Dignity	758,967	1.0
Stanislav Govorukhin	Independent	328,723	0.4
Yury Skuratov	Independent	319,189	0.4
Alexey Podberezkin	Spiritual Heritage	98,177	0.1
Umar Dzhabrailov	Independent	78,498	0.1
Against all		1,414,673	1.9
Invalid/blank votes		701,016	–
Total		75,070,770	100
Registered voters/turnout		109,372,043	68.6

2004

CANDIDATES	NOMINATING PARTIES	VOTES	%
Vladimir Putin	Independent	49,558,328	71.9
Nikolay Kharitonov	Communist Party	9,514,554	13.8
Sergey Glazyev	Independent	2,850,610	4.1
Irina Khakamada	Independent	2,672,189	3.9
Oleg Malyshkin	Liberal Democratic Party	1,405,326	2.0
Sergey Mironov	Russian Party of Life	524,332	0.8
Against all		2,397,140	3.5
Invalid/blank votes		578,847	–
Total		69,501,326	100
Registered voters/turnout		108,064,281	64.3

2008

CANDIDATES	NOMINATING PARTIES	VOTES	%
Dmitry Medvedev	United Russia	52,530,712	71.2
Gennady Zyuganov	Communist Party	13,243,550	18.0
Vladimir Zhirinovsky	Liberal Democratic Party	6,988,510	9.5
Andrei Bogdanov	Democratic Party	968,344	1.3
Invalid/blank ballots		1,105,533	–
Total		74,746,649	100
Registered voters/turnout		107,222,016	69.7

Source: Nohlen, Dieter and Philip Stöver, eds. *Elections in Europe: A Data Handbook.* Baden Baden: Nomos, 2010.

READING 103

Vladimir Putin on the War on Terror, 2004
Address in the Wake of the Beslan School Massacre

On the first day of grammar school across Russia, on September 1, 2004, Chechen separatists took hostage a school in southern Russia. The siege lasted three days. Over 1,100 people were held inside the school and 334 died. On the 4th (the day that Putin gave this speech), Russian security forces stormed the building with rockets, tanks, and heavy weapons. After the dust had settled, 186 children were dead. In the months that followed, the powers of law enforcement were expanded. The direct election of leaders in the various federated states was changed so that Russia's president would propose leaders who could then be approved by legislative bodies. Putin consolidated his control over the media and eliminated the election of State Duma members by direct vote. After reading this speech, what reasons do you think Putin had in offering up these words?

President Vladimir Putin: Speaking is hard. It is painful.

A terrible tragedy has taken place in our world. Over these last few days each and every one of us has suffered greatly and taken deeply to heart all that was happening in the Russian town of Beslan. There, we found ourselves confronting not just murderers, but people who turned their weapons against helpless children.

I would like now, first of all, to address words of support and condolence to those people who have lost what we treasure most in this life—our children, our loved and dear ones.

I ask that we all remember those who lost their lives at the hands of terrorists over these last days.

***

Russia has lived through many tragic events and terrible ordeals over the course of its history. Today, we live in a time that follows the collapse of a vast and great state, a state that, unfortunately, proved unable to survive in a rapidly changing world. But despite all the difficulties, we were able to preserve the core of what was once the vast Soviet Union, and we named this new country the Russian Federation.

We all hoped for change, change for the better. But many of the changes that took place in our lives found us unprepared. Why?

We are living at a time of an economy in transition, of a political system that does not yet correspond to the state and level of our society's development.

We are living through a time when internal conflicts and interethnic divisions that were once firmly suppressed by the ruling ideology have now flared up.

We stopped paying the required attention to defense and security issues and we allowed corruption to undermine our judicial and law enforcement system.

Furthermore, our country, formerly protected by the most powerful defense system along the length of its external frontiers overnight found itself defenseless both from the east and the west.

It will take many years and billions of rubles to create new, modern and genuinely protected borders.

But even so, we could have been more effective if we had acted professionally and at the right moment.

In general, we need to admit that we did not fully understand the complexity and the dangers of the processes at work in our own country and in the world. In any case, we proved unable to react adequately. We showed ourselves to be weak. And the weak get beaten.

Some would like to tear from us a "juicy piece of pie." Others help them. They help, reasoning that Russia still remains one of the world's major nuclear powers, and as such still represents a threat to them. And so they reason that this threat should be removed.

Terrorism, of course, is just an instrument to achieve these aims.

As I have said many times already, we have found ourselves confronting crises, revolts and terrorist acts on more than one occasion. But what has happened now, this crime committed by terrorists, is unprecedented in its inhumanness and cruelty. This is not a challenge to the President, Parliament or government. It is a challenge to all of Russia, to our entire people. Our country is under attack.

* * *

The terrorists think they are stronger than us. They think they can frighten us with their cruelty, paralyze our will and sow disintegration in our society.

It would seem that we have a choice—either to resist them or to agree to their demands. To give in, to let them destroy and plunder Russia in the hope that they will finally leave us in peace.

As the President, the head of the Russian state, as someone who swore an oath to defend this country and its territorial integrity, and simply as a citizen of Russia, I am convinced that in reality we have no choice at all. Because to allow ourselves to be blackmailed and succumb to panic would be to immediately condemn millions of people to an endless series of bloody conflicts like those of Nagorny Karabakh, Trans-Dniester and other similar tragedies. We should not turn away from this obvious fact.

What we are dealing with are not isolated acts intended to frighten us, not isolated terrorist attacks. What we are facing is direct intervention of international terror directed against Russia. This is a total, cruel and full-scale war that again and again is taking the lives of our fellow citizens.

World experience shows us that, unfortunately, such wars do not end quickly. In this situation we simply cannot and should not live in as carefree a manner as previously. We must create a much more effective security system and we must demand from our law enforcement agencies action that corresponds to the level and scale of the new threats that have emerged.

But most important is to mobilize the entire nation in the face of this common danger. Events in other countries have shown that terrorists meet the most effective resistance in places where they not only encounter the state's power but also find themselves facing an organized and united civil society.

* * *

Dear fellow citizens,

Those who sent these bandits to carry out this dreadful crime made it their aim to set our peoples against each other, put fear into the hearts of Russian citizens and unleash bloody interethnic strife in the

North Caucasus. In this connection I have the following words to say.

First, a series of measures aimed at strengthening our country's unity will soon be prepared. Second, I think it is necessary to create a new system of coordinating the forces and means responsible for exercising control over the situation in the North Caucasus. Third, we need to create an effective anti-crisis management system including entirely new approaches to the way the law enforcement agencies work.

I want to stress that all of these measures will be implemented in full accordance with our country's Constitution.

Dear friends,

We are living through very difficult and painful days. I would like now to thank all those who showed endurance and responsibility as citizens.

We were and always will be stronger than them, stronger through our morals, our courage and our sense of solidarity.

I saw this again last night.

In Beslan, which is literally soaked with grief and pain, people were showing care and support for each other more than ever.

They were not afraid to risk their own lives in the name of the lives and peace of others.

Even in the most inhuman conditions they remained human beings.

It is impossible to accept the pain caused by such loss, but these trials have brought us even closer together and have forced us to re-evaluate a lot of things.

Today we must be together, for it is only together that we will vanquish the enemy.

Source: Putin, Vladimir. "Address in the Wake of the Beslan School Massacre." September 4, 2004. Kremlin Presidential Transcripts. Copyright © (CC by 4.0) at http://en.kremlin.ru/events/president/transcripts/22589.

READING 104

Medvedev and Putin, 2008

This cartoon was printed in 2008 in Russia's most famous satirical newspaper, *Krokodil* (*Crocodile*). Even at the height of Stalin's repression in the 1930s, *Krokodil* found ways to spoof the Soviet power structure and the internal contradictions of Russian society. It has remained true to form in the post-Soviet era, and this caption is a fine example of modern Soviet satire. In 2007, the outgoing two-term president, Vladimir Putin, announced that he would support Dmitry Medvedev's campaign for election. Medvedev's approval ratings soared as he then announced that he would make Vladimir Putin the Prime Minister of the Russian government if he should win. Election posters showed the two men over the slogan, "Together we win!" and on March 2, 2008, Medvedev won. Go back to the election results provided in an earlier excerpt in this chapter. Compare them to Putin's results four years earlier. Now compare that to this cartoon. The overt message of the cartoon is that Putin is teaching Medvedev how to run the country. Now have a closer look. What does the size difference between the two men mean? What does it mean that Putin's steering wheel is larger than Medvedev's (and will presumably stay larger)? Do the safety belts that the men are wearing carry some import? What does it mean that they are in a car (does it say something about the motion and direction of the country)? And what might we derive from the little bear hanging from the rear-view mirror?

Caption: "Remember, here is where the brake is, and here is the gas—In May you will get to drive."

Source: Eastview Information Services, *Krokodil* Archive. Translation by Margaret Peacock.

READING 105

The Crimean Crisis, 2014
Speech by Putin to the Russian State Duma

Russia annexed the Crimea from Ukraine in February–March, 2014. Russian soldiers in plain clothes took over the Supreme Council of Crimea and a pro-Russian government took over. On the day that Putin gave this speech, Crimea became a federal subject of the Russian federation despite its being a part of Ukraine for fifty years. This is a long excerpt that seems to offer Putin's version of Russian history in relation to its neighboring states. What justifications does Putin give in this speech for the decision to annex Ukraine? What vision of the modern world does Putin paint here? Who is his audience and what message is he trying to convey?

Federation Council members, State Duma deputies, good afternoon. Representatives of the Republic of Crimea and Sevastopol are here among us, citizens of Russia, residents of Crimea and Sevastopol!

Dear friends, we have gathered here today in connection with an issue that is of vital, historic significance to all of us. A referendum was held in Crimea on March 16 in full compliance with democratic procedures and international norms.

More than 82 percent of the electorate took part in the vote. Over 96 percent of them spoke out in favor of reuniting with Russia. These numbers speak for themselves.

To understand the reason behind such a choice it is enough to know the history of Crimea and what Russia and Crimea have always meant for each other.

Everything in Crimea speaks of our shared history and pride. This is the location of ancient Khersones, where Prince Vladimir was baptised. His spiritual feat of adopting Orthodoxy predetermined the overall basis of the culture, civilisation and human values that unite the peoples of Russia, Ukraine and Belarus. The graves of Russian soldiers whose bravery brought Crimea into the Russian empire are also in Crimea. This is also Sevastopol—a legendary city with an outstanding history, a fortress that serves as the birthplace of Russia's Black Sea Fleet. Crimea is Balaklava and Kerch, Malakhov Kurgan and Sapun Ridge. Each one of these places is dear to our hearts, symbolizing Russian military glory and outstanding valor …

After the revolution, the Bolsheviks, for a number of reasons—may God judge them—added large sections of the historical South of Russia to the Republic of Ukraine. This was done with no consideration for the ethnic make-up of the population, and today these areas form the southeast of Ukraine

What matters now is that this decision was made in clear violation of the constitutional norms that were in place even then. The decision was made behind the scenes. Naturally, in a totalitarian state nobody bothered to ask the citizens of Crimea and Sevastopol. They were faced with the fact ...

Unfortunately, what seemed impossible became a reality. The USSR fell apart. Things developed so swiftly that few people realized how truly dramatic those events and their consequences would be. Many people both in Russia and in Ukraine, as well as in other republics hoped that the Commonwealth of Independent States that was created at the time would become the new common form of statehood ... It was only when Crimea ended up as part of a different country that Russia realized that it was not simply robbed, it was plundered.

Now, many years later, I heard residents of Crimea say that back in 1991 they were handed over like a sack of potatoes. This is hard to disagree with. And what about the Russian state? What about Russia? It humbly accepted the situation. This country was going through such hard times then that realistically it was incapable of protecting its interests. However, the people could not reconcile themselves to this outrageous historical injustice. All these years, citizens and many public figures came back to this issue, saying that Crimea is historically Russian land and Sevastopol is a Russian city. Yes, we all knew this in our hearts and minds, but we had to proceed from the existing reality and build our good-neighbourly relations with independent Ukraine on a new basis. Meanwhile, our relations with Ukraine, with the fraternal Ukrainian people have always been and will remain of foremost importance for us ...

Time and time again attempts were made to deprive Russians of their historical memory, even of their language and to subject them to forced assimilation. Moreover, Russians, just as other citizens of Ukraine are suffering from the constant political and state crisis that has been rocking the country for over 20 years.

I understand why Ukrainian people wanted change. They have had enough of the authorities in power during the years of Ukraine's independence. Presidents, prime ministers and parliamentarians changed, but their attitude to the country and its people remained the same. They milked the country, fought among themselves for power, assets and cash flows and did not care much about the ordinary people. They did not wonder why it was that millions of Ukrainian citizens saw no prospects at home and went to other countries to work as day laborers. I would like to stress this: it was not some Silicon Valley they fled to, but to become day laborers. Last year alone almost 3 million people found such jobs in Russia. According to some sources, in 2013 their earnings in Russia totaled over $20 billion, which is about 12% of Ukraine's GDP.

...

Colleagues, Our western partners, led by the United States of America, prefer not to be guided by international law in their practical policies, but by the rule of the gun. They have come to believe in their exclusivity and exceptionalism, that they can decide the destinies of the world, that only they can ever be right. They act as they please: here and there, they use force against sovereign states, building coalitions based on the principle "If you are not with us, you are against us." To make this aggression look legitimate, they force the necessary resolutions from international organizations, and if for some reason this does not work, they simply ignore the UN Security Council and the UN overall.

There was a whole series of controlled "colour" revolutions. Clearly, the people in those nations, where these events took place, were sick of tyranny and poverty, of their lack of prospects; but these feelings were taken advantage of cynically. Standards were imposed on these nations that did not in any way correspond to their way of life, traditions, or these peoples' cultures. As a result, instead of democracy and freedom, there was chaos, outbreaks in violence and a series of upheavals. The Arab Spring turned into the Arab Winter.

A similar situation unfolded in Ukraine. In 2004, to push the necessary candidate through at the presidential elections, they thought up some sort of third round that was not stipulated by the law. It was absurd and a mockery of the constitution. And now, they have thrown in an organised and well-equipped army of militants.

We understand what is happening; we understand that these actions were aimed against Ukraine and Russia and against Eurasian integration. And all this while Russia strived to engage in dialogue with our colleagues in the West. We are constantly proposing cooperation on all key issues; we want to strengthen our level of trust and for our relations to be equal, open and fair. But we saw no reciprocal steps …

In short, we have every reason to assume that the infamous policy of containment, led in the 18th, 19th and 20th centuries, continues today. They are constantly trying to sweep us into a corner because we have an independent position, because we maintain it and because we call things like they are and do not engage in hypocrisy. But there is a limit to everything. And with Ukraine, our western partners have crossed the line, playing the bear and acting irresponsibly and unprofessionally …

Today, it is imperative to end this hysteria, to refute the rhetoric of the cold war and to accept the obvious fact: Russia is an independent, active participant in international affairs; like other countries, it has its own national interests that need to be taken into account and respected.

At the same time, we are grateful to all those who understood our actions in Crimea; we are grateful to the people of China, whose leaders have always considered the situation in Ukraine and Crimea taking into account the full historical and political context, and greatly appreciate India's reserve and objectivity.

Today, I would like to address the people of the United States of America, the people who, since the foundation of their nation and adoption of the Declaration of Independence, have been proud to hold freedom above all else. Isn't the desire of Crimea's residents to freely choose their fate such a value? Please understand us …

I also want to address the people of Ukraine. I sincerely want you to understand us: we do not want to harm you in any way, or to hurt your national feelings. We have always respected the territorial integrity of the Ukrainian state, incidentally, unlike those who sacrificed Ukraine's unity for their political ambitions. They flaunt slogans about Ukraine's greatness, but they are the ones who did everything to divide the nation. Today's civil standoff is entirely on their conscience. I want you to hear me, my dear friends. Do not believe those who want you to fear Russia, shouting that other regions will follow Crimea. We do not want to divide Ukraine; we do not need that. As for Crimea, it was and remains a Russian, Ukrainian, and Crimean-Tatar land.

Let me say one other thing too. Millions of Russians and Russian-speaking people live in Ukraine and will continue to do so. Russia will always defend their interests using political, diplomatic and legal means. But it should be above all in Ukraine's own interest to ensure that these people's rights and interests are fully protected. This is the guarantee of Ukraine's state stability and territorial integrity.

Source: Putin, Vladimir. "Speech to the Russian State Duma." March 18, 2014. Kremlin Presidential Transcripts. Copyright © (CC by 4.0) at http://en.kremlin.ru/events/president/transcripts/22589.

READING 106

NATO Commander Reports on Russian Invasion of Ukraine, 2014

> In this excerpt, the commander of NATO in Europe, Curtis Scaparrotti, reports on the state of affairs in Ukraine. What are the implications of what he says here? What are each side's concerns de and what was the international and political significance of this?

Across the last few days, we have seen the same thing that OSCE [Organization for Security and Cooperation in Europe] is reporting. We have seen columns of Russian equipment, primarily Russian tanks, Russian artillery, Russian air defense systems, and Russian combat troops entering into Ukraine. We do not have a good picture at this time of how many. We agree that there are multiple columns that we have seen. We agree with the OSCE reports. And as to their intent, I am not sure. What worries me the most, I have said before, is that we have a situation where the former international border, the current international border of Ukraine and Russia, is completely porous. It is completely wide open. Forces, money, support, supplies, weapons, are flowing back and forth across this border completely at will, and that is not a good situation. We need to get back to a situation where this international border is respected, and that will help us to contain the problem of resupply into eastern Ukraine.

Source: Scaparrotti, Curtis. Report. *New York Times video*. November 12, 2014. Transcribed by Margaret Peacock.

READING 107

Putin Responds to Accusations of Russian Interference in the US 2016 Presidential Election, 2016

Vladimir Putin's Annual News Conference

In the months before the U.S. Presidential election, many in the West expressed concern that Russia was trying to sway how Americans voted. Here is Putin's response to the accusations of Russian meddling immediately after the election ended. What does this response say about the state of Russia and its future prospects in the years to come?

STEVEN ROSENBERG

Mr. President, your country has been accused of state-sponsored hacking with the aim of influencing the results of the US presidential election. And President Obama has hinted very strongly, he thinks that you are behind that. He said that not much happens in Russia without Vladimir Putin. And President Obama revealed that he told you personally to cut it out. So, what did you tell him in response? And can you confirm that you were warned by Washington not to tamper with America's election, warned in a message via the so-called Red Phone, the crisis line between your two countries?

VLADIMIR PUTIN

As concerns interference and what we discussed with President Obama. You may have noticed that I never speak about the private conversations I have with my colleagues.

First, about the interference. I already responded to one of your fellow journalists from the United States. The defeated party always tries to blame somebody on the outside. They should be looking for these problems closer to home.

Everybody keeps forgetting the most important point. For example, some hackers breached email accounts of the US Democratic Party leadership. Some hackers did that. But, as the President-elect rightly noted, does anyone know who those hackers were? Maybe they came from another country, not Russia. Maybe somebody just did it from their couch or bed. These days, it is very easy to designate a random country as the source of attack while being in a completely different location.

But is this important? I think the most important thing is the information that the hackers revealed to the public. Did they compile or manipulate the data? No, they did not. What is the best proof that the hackers uncovered truthful information? The proof is that after the hackers demonstrated how public opinion had been manipulated within the Democratic Party, against one candidate rather than the other, against candidate Sanders, the Democratic National Committee Chairperson resigned. This means she admitted that the hackers revealed the truth. Instead of apologizing to the voters and saying, "Forgive us, our bad, we will never do this again," they started yelling about who was behind the attacks. Is that important?

Source: Putin, Vladimir. Annual News Conference. December 23, 2016. Kremlin Presidential Transcripts. Copyright © (CC by 4.0) at http://en.kremlin.ru/events/president/transcripts/22589.

READING 108

U.S. Office of National Intelligence Report on Russian Hacking in the 2016 U.S. Presidential Elections, 2017

Read this report from the US National Intelligence Community. What conclusions does it draw about the extent of Russian interference in the U.S. Presidential election? As of the publication of this book, the investigation into Russian meddling continues. Given the catastrophic state of Russia in 1991, what is the significance of this document and the potential influence of Russia globally?

KEY JUDGMENTS

Russian efforts to influence the 2016 US presidential election represent the most recent expression of Moscow's longstanding desire to undermine the US-led liberal democratic order, but these activities demonstrated a significant escalation in directness, level of activity, and scope of effort compared to previous operations.

We assess Russian President Vladimir Putin ordered an influence campaign in 2016 aimed at the US presidential election. Russia's goals were to undermine public faith in the US democratic process, denigrate Secretary Clinton, and harm her electability and potential presidency. We further assess Putin and the Russian Government developed a clear preference for President-elect Trump. We have high confidence in these judgments.

- We also assess Putin and the Russian Government aspired to help President-elect Trump's election chances when possible by discrediting Secretary Clinton and publicly contrasting her unfavorably to him. All three agencies agree with this judgment. CIA and FBI have high confidence in this judgment; NSA has moderate confidence.
- Moscow's approach evolved over the course of the campaign based on Russia's understanding of the electoral prospects of the two main candidates. When it appeared to Moscow that Secretary Clinton was likely to win the election, the Russian influence campaign began to focus more on undermining her future presidency ...

Moscow's influence campaign followed a Russian messaging strategy that blends covert intelligence operations—such as cyber activity—with overt efforts by Russian Government agencies, state-funded media, third-party intermediaries, and paid social media users or "trolls." Russia, like its Soviet predecessor, has a history of conducting covert influence campaigns focused on US presidential elections that have used intelligence officers and agents and press placements to disparage candidates perceived as hostile to the Kremlin.

- We assess with high confidence that Russian military intelligence (General Staff Main Intelligence Directorate or GRU) used the Guccifer 2.0 persona and DCLeaks.com to release US victim data obtained in cyber operations publicly and in exclusives to media outlets and relayed material to WikiLeaks.
- Russian intelligence obtained and maintained access to elements of multiple US state or local electoral boards. DHS [Department of Homeland Security] assesses that the types of systems Russian actors targeted or compromised were not involved in vote tallying …

We assess Moscow will apply lessons learned from its Putin-ordered campaign aimed at the US presidential election to future influence efforts worldwide, including against US allies and their election processes.

Source: Office of the Director of National Intelligence. "Assessing Russian Activities and Intentions in Recent US Elections." ICA 2017–01D, Jan 6, 2017.

Printed in the USA
CPSIA information can be obtained
at www.ICGtesting.com
LVHW020927090823
754690LV00011B/33